The
CONQUERING
CANADIENS

Stanley Cup
Champions

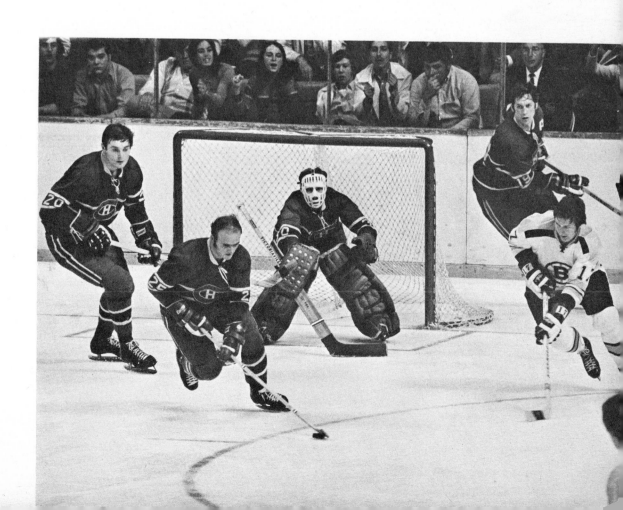

The CONQUERING CANADIENS

Stanley Cup Champions

by Stan Fischler
Photography by Dan Baliotti

A Stuart L. Daniels Book

PRENTICE-HALL OF CANADA, LTD.
Scarborough, Ontario

THE CONQUERING CANADIENS: Stanley Cup Champions
by Stan Fischler and Dan Baliotti

Published by
Prentice-Hall of Canada, Ltd.,
Scarborough, Ontario

ISBN 0-13-167775-6
Library of Congress Catalog Card Number:
75-183587

Prentice-Hall, Inc., Englewood Cliffs, New
Jersey
Prentice-Hall International, Inc., London
Prentice-Hall of Australia, Pty. Ltd., Sydney
Prentice-Hall of India Private Ltd., New
Delhi
Prentice-Hall of Japan, Inc., Tokyo

Printed in Canada

DEDICATION

To our mothers, our biggest and best critics.

ACKNOWLEDGMENTS

The authors wish to thank Vincent Claps, Bob Rush, Shirley Fischler, Al Robbins, Frank Brown, Nancy Demmon and Cary Howard who helped so much in the preparation of this book.

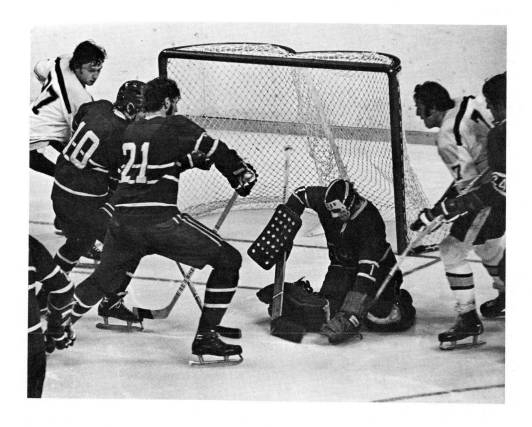

Dedication, excellence . . . the Canadiens

To understand professional hockey one has to understand the Montreal Canadiens. For it is Les Canadiens, more than any other team, which personifies the dedication, combativeness, competitiveness and excellence that makes hockey different from all other sports.

They have consistently produced the brightest of hockey stars—Morenz . . . Vezina . . . Richard . . . Beliveau . . . Harvey . . . Geoffrion . . . Durnan . . . Lach . . . Reardon . . . Bouchard—all of them members of hockey's hall of Fame, many of them hockey legend.

When he assumed the presidency of the club in 1957, Senator Hartland Molson said, "We don't own the Canadiens, really. The public of Montreal, in fact the entire province of Quebec, owns the Canadiens. The club is more than a professional sports organization. It is an institution, a way of life."

That's true enough, but he might have gone even further because the influence of the Canadiens on the National Hockey League extends far beyond Montreal and Quebec. The Canadiens have been the most successful of all National Hockey League teams; they have won the Stanley Cup 17 times, more often than any of their rivals and, since 1949, have been shut out of the championship competition only once.

The winning of the Cup in 1971 after the disastrous 1969–70 season proved once again the determined excellence of the team. But how did 1969–70 happen? Could it happen again?

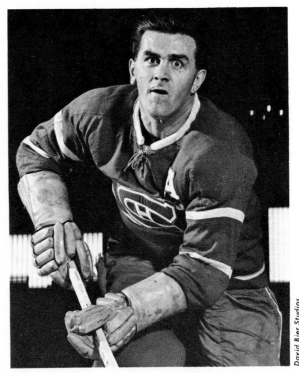

Maurice "The Rocket" Richard, former Canadiens' captain.

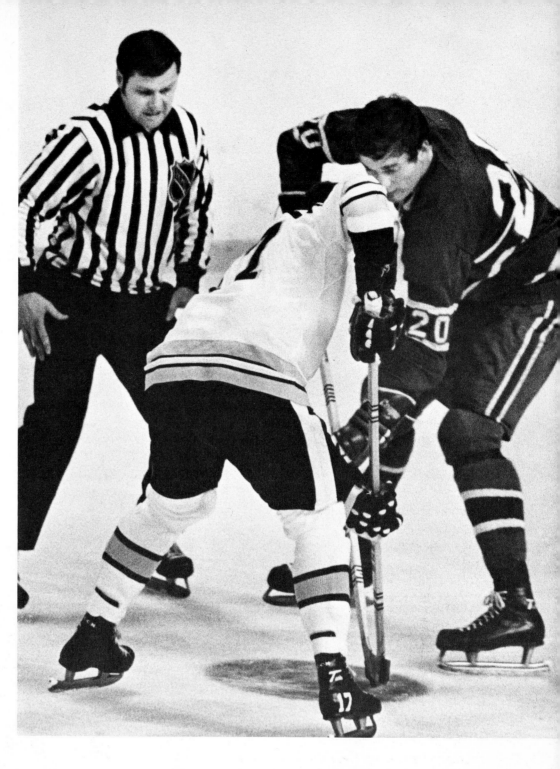

Peter "Little M" Mahovlich takes the face-off from Boston's Fred Stanfield.

Dark Days of Defeat

At the end of the 1968–69 season, and despite Montreal's Stanley Cup victory, coach Claude Ruel was enough of a realist to know that to be on solid ground he would have to lead the Canadiens to another Stanley Cup. On paper, they should be able to repeat their triumph. But then unfortunate things started to happen.

Captain Jean Beliveau, who had spent a good part of the summer expanding a successful public-relations firm, arrived in training camp exhausted from his outside business interests and stayed below par for the entire season. John Ferguson was plagued by injuries. Gilles Tremblay finally surrendered to a chronic asthma condition and retired. On top of that, the all-important goaltending fell apart. Gump Worsley and Rogatien Vachon had been solid in the nets all during the 1968–69 season and to back them up Ruel had Phillipe Myre, a young French-Canadian of great promise. But Myre failed to live up to expectations. The Canadiens soon regretted leaving Tony Esposito unprotected in the 1969 league draft. Chicago had claimed him, and at the conclusion of the 1969–70 season, Esposito was voted the league's All-Star goalie.

A wall of Chicago players block Jean Beli-veau from scoring while teammate Yvan Cournoyer looks on from the right.

Worse still, Ruel was having trouble controlling some of his players. It wasn't downright dissension, but some players made no secret of their disdain for Ruel, a situation that never would have occurred under former coach Toe Blake, now club vice president. A few of Ruel's more outspoken critics were sent packing, but still the problems persisted and the Canadiens floundered.

In defense of Claude Ruel, it should be said that the Canadiens of 1969–70 were not that bad a hockey club. The race in the East Division was one of the closest in memory, and while the Canadiens were never on top, they were never worse than third, either. But these were Les Canadiens, and anything less than total victory is unacceptable. It is a matter of pride.

Finally, in late February of 1970, Ruel offered to step aside, believing that perhaps his departure would weld the team together and enable the Canadiens to salvage the season.

"It's going to be tough to make first place now," Ruel said. "They can't do it by taking eighteen players from the Voyageurs (a Montreal farm club) but they can replace one man. I think enough of the team to want that, if it will help. With someone else behind the bench, the players that are not working now may decide to prove something."

Ruel's tacit admission that not all of the Canadiens were going all-out pointed up one of the team's basic and lingering problems. But he declined to name names.

"When you push and push your players and there's no improvement, something must be wrong," Ruel continued. "I'm no detective but I know something is wrong when some fellows feel like playing one night and leave it up to the other guys in the next game."

Ruel Stays

General manager Sam Pollock, noting that the team had suffered a number of injuries, declined to accept Ruel's offer to resign. He also had some sharp words about the attitude of Montreal fans.

"They've become spoiled by success," Pollock said. "Sometimes it seems they're rooting harder for the visiting club than they are for us. This has to have an effect on our club, and it might explain why we've done so poorly at The Forum and so well on the road."

On March 10, 1970 the Canadiens dropped into fifth place. They had lost on successive nights to Detroit and Boston and there were now demands—from sportswriters and from fans—that Ruel be dismissed. Beliveau rushed to his defense.

"It is ridiculous to blame the coach," Jean Beliveau said. "He is the same coach we had last season. The players themselves are to blame. We know what has to be done. We've done it before. We don't need to be told. And it is a fact—I haven't been producing."

A few days later Ruel was signed to a contract for the 1970–71 season. Meanwhile, the Canadiens had defeated the New York Rangers, 5–3, in a crucial game at The Forum, but in the process lost defenseman Serge Savard with a broken leg. With Savard gone, Ruel turned to John Ferguson and he responded with two fine efforts on the weekend of March 14 and 15. The Canadiens beat the Blues in St. Louis and tied Toronto in that city. Montreal was on the move.

A week later the Canadiens vaulted over the Rangers into fourth place. And a few days after that they defeated the Maple Leafs and moved into third place. Ahead lay a home-and-home series with the Rangers. A win in either game would all but assure the Canadiens of a playoff berth.

The first of those two games was played in The Forum. It was a scoreless match until 11:27 of the third period, when Peter Mahovlich scored while the Canadiens were on a power play. But with less than three minutes to play, Walter Tkaczuk beat Vachon from close range and the game ended in a 1–1 tie. On the following night, in New York, the Rangers dominated the play from start to finish and won, 4–1. The Canadiens were in trouble again. But following their loss the Canadiens beat the Bruins in Boston and so entered the final weekend of play just 3 points out of first place and 2 points ahead of the fifth-place Rangers.

Speeding past Boston defenseman Don Awrey, Cournoyer moves toward the Bruins' goal.

With goalie Tony Esposito behind him, Yvan waits for a pass during the NHL All-Star Game.

Montreal was finishing its schedule with a home-and-home series against the Chicago Black Hawks, who were tied with the Bruins for first place. The Rangers were finishing with a home-and-home series against fourth-place Detroit. Montreal lost its first game to Chicago, 4–1. But the Rangers also lost, and so the Canadiens retained their 2-point lead wth one game to play. It now seemed impossible for them to finish out of the playoffs.

The Impossible Happens

The impossible happened. New York's game against Detroit was in the afternoon. Playing for the most part against patchwork lines, the Rangers bombed the Wings by a score of 9–5. Suddenly the Canadiens were in trouble. For if Montreal and New York finished with identical records, as would be the case if the Canadiens lost to Chicago, the team with the most goals during the season would be awarded fourth place. And the Rangers, by virtue of their 9 goals, now held a 4-goal lead in that suddenly all-important category.

Against Chicago, the Canadiens scored first. But before the first period was over the Hawks had 2 goals, and with ten minutes left in the game Montreal trailed, 5–2. At that point Ruel pulled his goaltender in an effort to get enough goals to surpass the Rangers. However, Esposito turned aside every Montreal thrust while the Hawks hit the open net five times in the final nine minutes. Montreal went down to an ignominious 10–2 defeat. For the first time since 1948 the Canadiens had failed to make the playoffs. 'It's like a bad dream,'' said Henri Richard, and that seemed to say it all.

Two days later the owners and executives of the Canadiens called a news conference. Toe Blake was critical of the manner in which Detroit had played its last game against the Rangers. Pollock was, too, but he did not dwell on Detroit. Instead, he blamed the Canadiens' terrible season on the Canadiens.

"We lost," Pollock said. "It's not just one game, it's a whole season that decides it. That's the crux of the whole bloody thing."

A New Season—Another Chance

The next season was to be something else again. A lesser team might have been demoralized by a fifth-place finish after a glorious two decades. Not the Canadiens.

Before the start of the 1970–71 season, there were two important developments affecting the team: Al MacNeil was hired to assist Claude Ruel and John Ferguson retired. Knowledgeable hockey people regarded Ferguson as the "heart" of the Canadiens. Besides providing inspiration, he also provided muscle. He would be missed.

Montreal opened its season against Detroit and beat the Red Wings, 4–3. Yvan Cournoyer led the attack with two goals and an assist. Vachon was in goal and overall the Canadiens looked stronger than they had at the conclusion of the 1969–70 campaign. But it soon became apparent that under Ruel, Montreal was a third-place team. And so twenty-three games into the 1970–71 season, Ruel was relieved as coach and replaced by MacNeil.

However, the Canadiens remained a third-place team. Injuries were partly responsible. Beliveau and Cournoyer were out for long stretches. Savard, trying to get back to peak form after breaking his leg near the end of the 1970 season, broke it again and was sidelined for the remainder of the campaign.

On the plus side, Ferguson came out of retirement. The Canadiens brought up a couple of rookies, Rejean Houle and Bobby Sheehan from the Voyageurs and they performed well. Montreal also acquired Frank Mahovlich from Detroit. In late February and early March the Canadiens made a move on second place, but the Rangers held them off and Montreal finished the season in third, with 97 points.

Oh, Yes—Dryden

Oh, yes. In March the Canadiens also brought up from the Voyageurs a young goalie named Ken Dryden. Twenty-three years old and a graduate of Cornell University, Dryden was the brother of goalie Dave Dryden, who had tended the nets for the Chicago Black Hawks and now played for the Buffalo Sabres. Before the season's end Dryden played in six games and the Canadiens won them all. MacNeil decided to open the playoffs with Dryden as goaltender. It was an astonishing ploy, like opening the World Series with a rookie pitcher.

Hockey's Greatest Upset

Montreal's first-round opponents in Stanley Cup play were the fearsome Boston Bruins, who had required only fourteen games to win the Cup the previous year. A lot of experts figured the Bruins might need only twelve games this time around.

Offensively, the Bruins were awesome. As a team they had scored 399 goals during regular-season play. Four players—Phil Esposito, Bobby Orr, Johnny Bucyk and Kenny Hodge—had each registered more than 100 points. Defensively, the Bruins were vulnerable, but what they lacked in defensive finesse they more than made up for in sheer ferocity. Boston is a physical team. The Bruins hit hard. They slam into corners. They beat on opponents. They intimidate people.

In regular-season play the Canadiens had lost five of six games to the Bruins. They had faced Boston twice on the final weekend of play and were beaten decisively both times. Little wonder, then, that the odds-makers made Boston a 4–1 favorite over Montreal. And the odds held up beautifully through the first game as Boston won it in routine fashion, 3–1. There was only one untoward incident. Midway through the third period, referee John Ashley called Orr for holding Yvan Cournoyer, and Orr exploded. Skating alongside the referee on the way to the penalty box Orr screamed, "You miss fourteen penalties on them and then call a cheap one on me."

As Orr stepped into the penalty box he continued to shout at Ashley and the referee promptly hit him with a ten-minute misconduct. Thoroughly enraged at that point, Orr charged out of the box, pushed linesman Ron Ego and started after Ashley. Had Orr reached Ashley and hit him he conceivably would have been suspended for a few play-off games and possibly the whole series. Fortunately for Orr, he was intercepted by six teammates and literally pushed back into the penalty box. Later, Ashley told reporters he hadn't seen Orr leave the box or push Ego. The case was closed and there would be no disciplinary action which moved one unidentified Canadien to say, "If it had been John Ferguson, he'd have been suspended for a few games."

For game number two, Bruin coach Tom Johnson, who had been an outstanding defenseman for Montreal in his playing days, switched goalies, starting Ed Johnston instead of Gerry Cheevers. With Johnston in the nets the

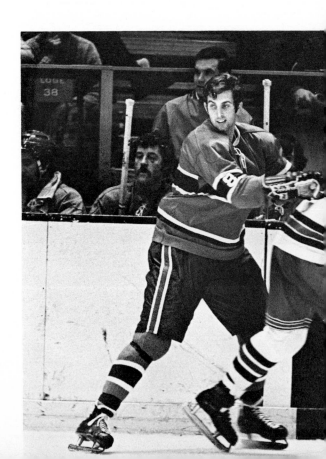

Bruins built a 5–2 lead in the first two periods. The score held at 5–1 until late in the second session when Henri Richard took the puck off Orr's stick inside the Boston zone and put it past the helpless Johnston. At the time, Richard's goal appeared meaningless. But for the Canadiens it proved inspirational.

Early in the third period Jean Beliveau scored a power-play goal and almost miraculously the Canadiens were only 2 goals down and flying. Moments later Ferguson wrestled the puck away from Orr in the Boston zone and put it on Beliveau's stick. With Dallas Smith draped over him, Jean maneuvered the puck onto his backhand and beat Johnston cleanly from close in.

The atmosphere in Boston Garden suddenly changed. Boston fans, who had rooted all year for the best team in hockey, sensed defeat. The "Montreal mystique" had taken over and it must have touched a responsive chord in the Boston players, for they let the Canadiens roll right over them.

Amazing

Jacques Lemaire tied the score at 5-all, breaking past the Boston defense and beating Johnston from close-in. Then, in a scramble behind the Boston net, Beliveau came up with the puck and slipped it onto the stick of Ferguson just outside the Boston crease. Ferguson shot and the Canadiens led, 6–5. Later, Frank Mahovlich broke away to score for Montreal, and that's the way the game ended, 7–5, Canadiens. Amazing!

"Psychologically, the Bruins have to remember what happened here," Beliveau said over the din in the delirious Montreal dressing room. "When you lose a 4-goal lead, you don't forget."

Derek Sanderson, Boston's pugnacious center, agreed. "That game hurt us, really hurt us," he said. "We lost our home-ice advantage. You should never blow a 4-goal lead in the playoffs."

For the first minutes of game three in The Forum, it appeared that the Bruins had erased the memory of their galling defeat. Twenty-nine seconds after the start of play Phil Esposito broke down the right wing and fired the puck from 30 feet out. Goalie Ken Dryden had handled far tougher chances in the first two games. This time the shot fooled him and Boston led, 1–0.

"I was just getting set for him (Esposito) but he shot from farther out than I expected," Dryden explained later. "The puck went off my pad and into the far side."

However, that was Dryden's only mistake of the night and Boston's only goal. Montreal, meanwhile, got 2 goals from Frank Mahovlich and a third from Jacques Laperriere. The game ended with Montreal on top, 3–1. Dryden had 37 saves.

"I think perhaps the Bruins thought we would lay down and die for them in the playoffs," Ferguson remarked. "But, hey, the Canadiens are proud. We don't play dead for anybody."

"What a nightmare," said Bobby Orr, "what a nightmare."

Yvan Cournoyer squeezes past Jim Neilson (left) and Bruce MacGregor of the New York Rangers.

In game four the Bruins came out flying. In the first period they fired thirteen shots at Dryden. He stopped them all. Montreal, meanwhile, managed only five shots against Cheevers, but made one of them pay off. With Dallas Smith off for holding, Jacques Lemaire fired a hard shot from the point and Frank Mahovlich was there to put in the rebound at 3:53. At one point during that first period the Bruins held a four-to-three manpower advantage for one minute and 49 seconds but could not score. Later, they had a five-three advantage for 41 seconds and again could not get on the board.

Then, early in the second period, Boston winger Mike Walton got into a skirmish with defenseman Terry Harper. Ferguson jumped in. He and Walton exchanged blows, then wrestled each other to the ice. There was no clear-cut winner in the fight, but it seemed to ignite the Bruins.

Two minutes later Orr skated into the Montreal zone and shot the puck at Dryden from 15 feet out and at a sharp angle. It caught the left-hand corner of the net just inside the post and the game was tied, 1—1. A few minutes later Dryden stopped Fred Stanfield on a breakaway and beat John McKenzie on the rebound. A minute after that he made a spectacular glove save off Orr on a slap shot. Still the Bruins came on, and when Phil Roberto was called for slashing they had a big power-play opportunity. Walton made good on it, hitting with a slap shot from the point at 18:26.

Thirty-seven seconds into the third period Orr scored again, this time on a 40-footer from directly in front of the cage. Cournoyer got that one back six minutes later, beating Cheevers on a short shot while using Orr as a screen. The Canadiens pressed from that point on but Cheevers held them off and Stanfield finally wrapped it up for the Bruins with a score at 17:21. Boston's fifth and final goal came at 19:57, Orr turning the "hat trick" by popping the puck into an empty net, as MacNeil had pulled Dryden in a futile attempt to get the tying goals in the final 90 seconds. So Boston had regained its home-ice advantage, and entering game number five they were again favored to win the series and march onward to the Stanley Cup.

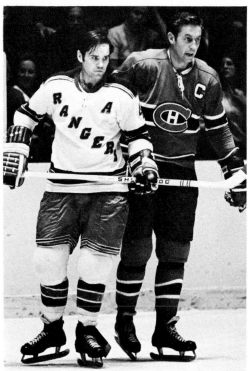

Game Five—Boston's Best

Game five was Boston's best. The Bruins outshot the Canadiens in that game, 56–27, and beat them, 7–3. In the first period alone the Bruins had 23 shots on goal and converted three of them for a 3–1 lead. Boston was hitting at both ends of the ice, and for the first time in the playoffs Dryden was beginning to wilt under Boston's enormous firepower. Boston added 2 more goals in the second period, one of them by Eddie Westfall while the Bruins were short-handed.

During the first few minutes of the third period, however, horrified Boston fans began to wonder if they were about to witness a replay of the second game. Early in the session Frank Mahovlich scored to make it a 5–2 game, and a few minutes later John Ferguson put a casually played puck behind Cheevers to cut the Boston lead to 2 goals. A minute later Jacques Lemaire found himself with the puck and an open net but fell down before he could shoot. That seemed to turn the tide. Montreal did not score again. Bucyk and Hodge did. And the Bruins were only one game away from disposing of the bothersome Canadiens.

Coach Al MacNeil insists that he did not give his team any special pep talk before the sixth game. "I just turned them loose and told them to go," MacNeil says. And "go" the Canadiens did.

Reversing the trend of previous games, Montreal outshot Boston, 11–5 in the first period. The Canadiens also outhustled and outhit the Bruins and left the ice with a 2–1 lead after the first 20 minutes of play. Peter Mahovlich and Richard scored for Montreal, while Esposito flipped a short backhander off Jacques Laperriere and past Dryden.

At 5:57 of the second period Fred Stanfield tied the game, but that proved to be Boston's last gasp. A few minutes later Cheevers was called for tripping, and 20 seconds after that penalty Bobby Orr was banished for holding the puck. With that two-man advantage Montreal broke the deadlock, Lemaire converting passes from Frank Mahovlich and J. C. Tremblay. Then, after Dryden had stopped first Esposito and then Orr on dangerous shots, Tremblay split defensemen Ted Green and Don Awrey, came in alone on Cheevers and put the puck behind him.

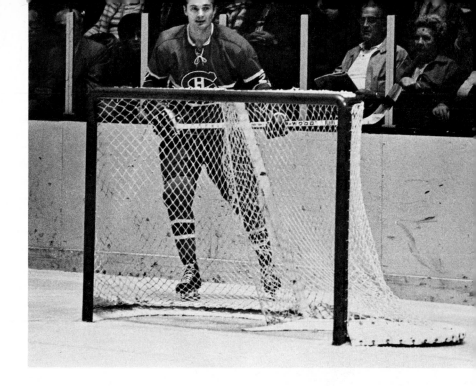

The final score was 8–3. Richard got his second goal of the game and so did Peter Mahovlich. On Mahovlich's second goal Dryden received an assist. That made him only the second goalie in Stanley Cup history to register a point. Toronto's Johnny Bower had picked up an assist against Montreal back in 1963. When Dryden's assist was announced, the 17,491 fans in The Forum responded with a standing ovation, one of the loudest and longest ever in that fabled hockey rink.

"At first I didn't realize it was for me," Dryden said later. "Then I figured it out, I guess, and it was a little embarrassing. It was Pete who got the goal, not me."

In the Montreal dressing room after the game, Canadien players were quiet but confident. "It's been there all the time," remarked captain Beliveau. "Tonight we just put it together—as a team—every last one of us. And there's no reason why we can't do it again."

Terry Harper looked up from unlacing his skates, grinned and asked reporters clustered around him, "Do you think that reports of the Bruins' invincibility might have been slightly premature?"

Over in the Boston dressing room coach Johnson was at a loss to explain his team's collapse. "But we've got to find out before Sunday," he said. "I'm still convinced we're a better team. We proved that over the schedule. This was easily our worst game of the year." But in the actions and the attitudes of the Boston players you could sense the beginning of self-doubt. "It's unreal," Sanderson remarked. "How do you explain it?"

Peter Mahovlich prior to a face-off.

The Telling Seventh

So it came down to game seven in the dilapidated Boston Garden. There was pressure, tremendous pressure on both teams. On the night before the game even the great Jean Beliveau awoke three times, each time staring at the ceiling and wondering how he would perform. In the darkness of the same night Ken Dryden awoke to find himself on his feet with arms outstretched and stiffened, as though to stop an opponent's shot. On the day of the game Phil Esposito stomped into the Boston dressing room. His face was glum. In his mind he kept hearing the words of team-mate Wayne Cashman, "This whole season, everything we have done, comes down to this final game."

At 6:50 of the first period Ken Hodge took advantage of a Montreal defensive lapse and flicked the puck past Dryden. The Bruins didn't lead for very long. Before the first period ended Frank Mahovlich scored, using his stick to bat a Lemaire pass out of the air, to capture the puck and put it past a startled Cheevers. Then Rejean Houle scored, rapping in the rebound of a Peter Mahovlich shot that had struck the goalpost. On both goals Cheevers was deserted by his defensemen.

In the second period J. C. Tremblay took a pass from Lemaire and beat Cheevers from 30 feet out. Then, just seconds after the start of the third period, Lemaire poked the puck off Orr's stick just inside the Boston blue line. He gave the puck to Frank Mahovlich and the Big M beat Cheevers. A minute later Johnny Bucyk scored for Boston, and now it was the Bruins against Dryden.

In the final eighteen minutes of the game they came at him in waves. He stopped Esposito. He stopped Orr. He stopped Bucyk. And then Esposito again, and still again. Phil, in frustration, slammed his stick against the Herculite glass behind the Montreal net. Unwittingly, it was a gesture of defeat. The Bruins were finished. The final score, 4–2.

"Their entire team played well," Esposito said after the game. "But Dryden decided the series. He never cracked, never appeared to lose confidence or be bothered by the pressure. He beat us."

In those seven games Dryden faced 286 Boston shots, an average of 41 a game. Just to have stood up under that barrage would have been remarkable in itself. To have emerged as the winning goalie in four of those seven games was incredible.

"I think it took a couple of games for our club to realize just how good we really are," Dryden said. "In the second game, we fell behind, 5–1, but no one quit. We came back to win it and that told us we had a chance to take the series."

"We played a helluva series," Al MacNeil said. "We beat a helluva team."

The Amazing Minnesota Challenge

Montreal's second-round series against the Minnesota North Stars should have been strictly a warmup for the finals against either the New York Rangers or the Chicago Black Hawks. Minnesota had finished fourth in the West Division, and while the North Stars had upset the St. Louis Blues in the first round of Cup play, few observers regarded them as a serious threat to the hot-handed Canadiens and their instant super goalie, Ken Dryden.

Not surprisingly, then, only 16,000 fans were in The Forum when the Canadiens and North Stars faced-off in game number one. There were a few anxious moments. Danny Grant scored the first goal of the game to give Minnesota a 1–0 lead. But it was short-lived. The Canadiens got stronger as the game wore on and coasted to a 7–2 win.

The second game, also in The Forum, was expected to develop along the same lines. But it didn't. At 5:14 of the first period, Jean-Paul Parise scored for the North Stars while John Ferguson was in the penalty box for tripping. Before the first session was over Jude Drouin, Ted Hampson and Lou Nanne also had scored and the North Stars led, 4–0. Stunned by the unexpected turn of events, the Canadiens came out flying in period number two. Peter Mahovlich scored at 4:17, and 12 minutes later Guy Lapointe beat Cesar Maniago to cut Minnesota's margin to 2 goals. But a minute later veteran Murray Oliver hit the net with a slap shot from just inside the blue line.

"I wasn't ready for it," Dryden later admitted. "It came at a bad time, just as the team was starting to rally. It was a bad, bad night."

Frank "Big M" Mahovlich takes a pass from Yvan Cournoyer in front of New York goalie Ed Giacomin.

Jean Beliveau scored for Montreal at 4:59 of the third period, but that was a last gasp. Charlie Burns made the final score 6–3 when his long drive deflected off Yvan Cournoyer into the net with just 24 seconds remaining.

John Ferguson had been watching the entire third period from the Montreal bench. Coach Al MacNeil had sat him down, presumably because John had been in the penalty box for 2 of Minnesota's first-period goals. Each time Ferguson's shift came up during the third period he showed his displeasure by banging his stick against the boards. When Burns netted Minnesota's sixth goal, Ferguson stormed off the Montreal bench and into the dressing room. On his way he paused to ram his fist into the stick rack.

Ferguson was back in the lineup for game number three as the series shifted to Minnesota. He contributed a goal and an assist and the Canadiens won easily, 6–3. Ferguson missed the fourth game because of an injury to his hip, however, and, coincidentally or not, the Canadiens lost, 5–2. That squared the series at two-all and the Canadiens were now more than embarrassed. They were plainly worried.

Most of the concern centered on Dryden, who had allowed 16 goals in the first four games. There was a feeling that he might have fallen into a slump after his outstanding series against Boston. Then, too, some of the Canadiens were starting to complain about MacNeil's juggling of lines. After the fourth-game loss, one Canadien (who declined to be identified) told reporters, "Well, there's one consolation in losing—we can look forward to the new lines next game."

The Crucial Fifth

For the Canadiens, then, the fifth game had become crucial. That in itself was a tribute to the North Stars. What's more, Minnesota came dangerously close to winning it. Over the first two periods the underdogs outshot Montreal, 18–11. But the North Stars were unable to score, partly because they were overeager, partly because Dryden was back in form. The Canadiens, meanwhile, had a 1-goal lead, the result of a Peter Mahovlich slap shot at 2:24 of the second period.

Montreal increased its lead to 2–0 at 1:14 of the third session, with Guy Lapointe steering the puck past Maniago from close range. But 26 seconds later Grant scored and

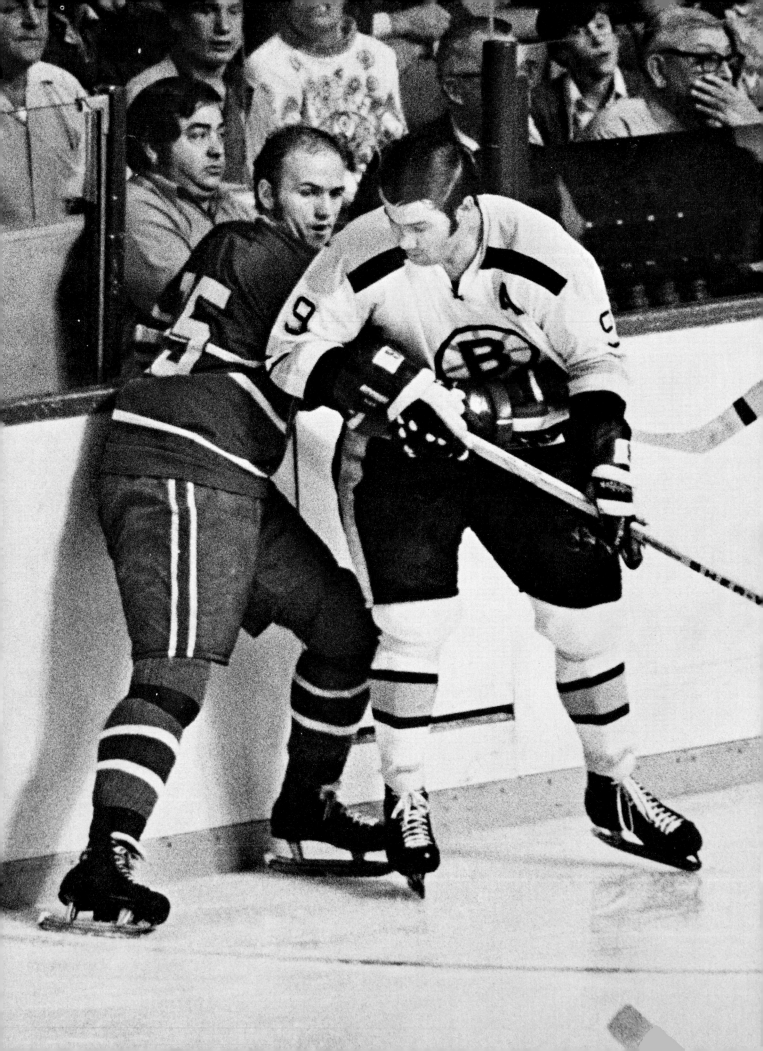

Montreal's margin was again just 1 goal. Then, at the six-minute mark, Hampson broke in alone on Dryden after receiving a great pass from ex-Canadien Bobby Rousseau. But Hampson's shot went into Dryden's pads.

"If Hampson had picked the corner of the net," Minnesota general-manager Wren Blair said later, "the score would have been 2–2."

At 9:49 Minnesota's Barry Gibbs was detected for tripping and just nineteen seconds later Peter Mahovlich tipped in Lapointe's 30-foot screamer. That broke the North Stars. In the next four-and-a-half minutes the Canadiens got goals from Ferguson, Frank Mahovlich and Cournoyer to win going away.

The Canadiens wrapped up the series in game number six at Minnesota. The final score was 3–2. That game will rank as one of the more memorable of Stanley Cup play because Ted Hampson shot the puck past Dryden for what would have been the tying goal just a split second after the green light went on, signaling the end of the game.

Montreal had gained the finals.

On to the Stanley Cup

From the standpoint of physical and mental readiness, the Canadiens and Black Hawks offered something of a contrast as they entered the Stanley Cup finals. The Canadiens had suffered physically at the hands of the Bruins, as does every team that takes them on, but even more important they had reached an emotional high in winning that first round against the highly favored league-leaders. With that upset behind them, Montreal suffered a natural letdown, which explained, in part, the unexpected difficulties they had in disposing of the North Stars. The question was, had Montreal lost its competitive edge?

The Black Hawks should have entered the series at their competitive peak. Chicago had swept Philadelphia in the first round with an ease that was almost embarrassing. Hull and company rode in on the Flyers' goal all but unchallenged. And at the other end of the ice Tony Esposito was seldom put to a severe test. But in the second round, against the Rangers, it was an entirely different story. The 1971 Chicago–New York series is regarded as one of the best in Stanley Cup history. The Hawks won in seven games. But two of those games were decided in overtime periods. A third game was settled in the third overtime period. The teams played almost two full games that night. In the seventh and deciding game Chicago rallied from a 2–1 deficit midway in the second period to win by a score of

4–2. The Hawks were exhausted after the Ranger series although not physically bruised. They were also high, mentally and competitively. That was one of the reasons the majority of experts picked Chicago to win the Stanley Cup. There were others.

Against the Rangers, Esposito had outplayed the league's All-Star goalie, Ed Giacomin. There was little reason to believe that Esposito would be any less effective against the Canadiens. True, Dryden had been spectacular against Boston. But he had been less than that against the North Stars. And with so little experience there was some doubt that he could withstand the pressure of a Stanley Cup final.

Then, too, in the New York series, Chicago's defensive tandem of Bill White and Pat Stapleton had shown that they ranked with the best. Finally, there was Bobby Hull. He had scored 2 winning goals against the Rangers—one in overtime and the second in the seventh game. Yet, those were Hull's only two goals. The Rangers had come close to neutralizing Hull by assigning him a shadow—Bob Nevin for the most part, Ron Stewart occasionally. Montreal had its own shadow ready—twenty-one-year-old Rejean Houle. But again there was the question of whether a relatively inexperienced youngster like Houle could handle the likes of Bobby Hull.

The Series Opens

The series opened in Chicago on May 4. Outside Chicago Stadium it was hot and humid. Inside, the 20,000 fans who took up every available seat and just about every inch of standing room roared a raucous welcome as the Black Hawks skated onto the ice. For the Canadiens, a chorus of boos. Nothing personal. That's just the way of a Chicago hockey crowd.

There was no scoring in the first period. Each team seemed to be feeling out the other. Both appeared sharp. "I was worried about the game for about the first couple of minutes," Chicago coach Billy Reay said later, "and then I knew we were ready."

Vic Hadfield of New York proves to Dryden
that you can't stop 'em all.

The Hawks did have the better of play in the first period. Dryden was called on to make some tough saves. The second period, however, was different. Les Habitants came out flying and the Hawks quickly became disorganized. As Montreal continued to put pressure on Esposito it seemed only a matter of time until the Canadiens would break through. Finally, they did, on a picture-play goal by Lemaire. And the way they were playing it appeared they could hold Chicago scoreless and net a few more goals.

But in the third period the game turned around again. Suddenly the Hawks were pressing. Dryden made some spectacular saves, but again there was that feeling of inevitability, the feeling that Chicago would break through before the game was over. Just before the midway point of the period, Bobby Hull scored and the game was tied.

It stayed that way through the rest of the third period. Jim Pappin had a chance to win it for the Hawks late in the session but Dryden stopped him from in close. Early in the first overtime period, Frank Mahovlich came close for the Canadiens, but Esposito stopped *him*. Overall, though, Chicago held the edge in play, while the Canadiens seemed to grow less certain and more tired as the game wore on.

Then, one minute into the second overtime period, Pappin carried the puck across the Montreal blue line. Yvan Cournoyer and Terry Harper leveled him with a vicious bodycheck and, as Pappin fell to the ice, the puck skidded free, to the right side of the Montreal net. Stan Mikita got to it first. As two Canadiens converged on Mikita and Pappin regained his feet, Stan moved in on Dryden.

"I gave Dryden every fake I knew," Mikita said later.

"He (Mikita) had the puck seven or eight feet in front," Dryden said later. "I didn't see Pappin at all."

But Mikita did. He shoveled a pass to Pappin, who shot the puck into the net at 1:11.

"As soon as Mikita passed it, I sprawled," Dryden said. "But it was much too late."

For Dryden it was an especially heartbreaking defeat. He had stopped 56 Chicago shots. In the Montreal dressing room there was a sense of gloom, but certainly the Canadiens were far from disheartened.

The tension of waiting—Ken Dryden.

A Goalies Game

"The goalies certainly dominated this game," MacNeil remarked to reporters. "There were some great saves out there. But overtime is one big play, a mistake by one side and it's all over." Then, referring to Chicago's overall home-ice advantage, since, if the series went to seven games, four would be in Chicago, MacNeil added, "We've got to get one game here."

For a time it looked as though the Canadiens would "get one game" in the second match. The Hawks had scored first, Bobby Hull putting the puck behind Dryden during a power play. The Canadiens bounced back with 2 before the first period was over—a power-play goal by Lemaire and a score by Peter Mahovlich. Mahovlich's goal was especially pretty, as he "deked" Esposito to the ice and then put the puck behind him with a sharp backhand shot. And the Canadiens continued to dominate the play early in the second period and might have gone on to win had it not been for Chicago's favorite "utility" player, Lou Angotti.

His first contribution went unnoticed by many. Early in the second period Chico Maki let fly with a long shot from just inside the Montreal blue line. Dryden barely moved as the puck flew past him and into the net.

"I wouldn't have had the goal if it wasn't for Lou," Maki would say later. "He set up the perfect screen for me."

With that quick, unexpected goal, the momentum shifted to the Black Hawks. Less than two minutes after Maki's goal Pappin scored, so at the end of two periods Chicago led, 3–2.

Early in the third period it was still anyone's game. Then, a clearing pass by J. C. Tremblay bounced off the boards and onto Angotti's stick. Lou shot and the Hawks were 2 goals up. Frank Mahovlich cut the margin to 1 with his twelfth score of the playoffs, only to have Angotti put the game out of reach with his second goal following a steal of the puck from Tremblay in the Montreal zone.

"When I got control of the puck I thought I was too close to Dryden," Angotti said in describing his second goal after Chicago's 5–3 victory. "Dryden came out and when I made a move to the right, he didn't move. So I shot. Usually I fall on my face on plays like that."

Frank Mahovlich to the attack.

In the Montreal dressing room Tremblay was philosophical about his errors. "I've made mistakes before," he said. "I don't brood over them. I have no excuses. He just made a good play. You could say I made a star out of Angotti."

By now the Canadiens realized that their situation was serious, although not critical. The next two games were at The Forum.

"We were overcautious in the overtime of the first game," MacNeil said. "We started the second game well, taking it to them and controlling play, but we seemed to go flat and the Hawks took it away from us.

"You need 60 minutes together in this game," Mac-Neil added. "You've got to work extra hard against a team like this. You can't make mistakes."

Chicago's Billy Reay was cautious: "Don't kid yourself. Those Montrealers aren't out of this yet." Jean Beliveau agreed: "We've been in this position before. We have come back before and we can come back again."

For the first period of the third game it appeared that "Le Gros Bill" would prove to be a prophet without honor. The Canadiens were flat, the Black Hawks confident. Montreal had shots on goal, but could not mount a sustained attack. Canadiens' defensemen were hesitant. Even Dryden looked somewhat uncertain.

The Hawks Score

At 3:09 of the first period Peter Mahovlich was called for elbowing and the Hawks quickly capitalized on their manpower advantage. Mikita started the scoring play by taking the puck from defenseman Guy Lapointe along the right boards deep in Montreal ice. He sent the puck to Bobby Hull on the right point. Hull faked a slap shot, then slid the puck to Cliff Koroll, who was skating right-to-left toward the Montreal goal. Koroll fired from fifteen feet out and Dryden didn't have a chance.

Ten minutes later the Hawks scored again. In that instance Pit Martin passed from the right point to Pappin,

The pause that refreshes.

34

who was stationed to the left of the Montreal goal. Pappin backhanded the puck to the goalmouth and Bobby Hull jammed it home. That was Hull's last goal of the series. No one knew it at the time, of course. What's more, even though Chicago was outshot in the first period, 13–8, it looked as if the Hawks were in complete control of the game. But it only looked that way.

"It's kind of tough to outshoot them in the first period and come up empty," Peter Mahovlich said later. "But we decided we wouldn't stay empty and we didn't." MacNeil talked to his players between periods and told them to "keep skating and keep driving because we were out-shooting them and something had to happen."

Peter Mahovlich made something happen at 5:56 of the second period. He took the puck away from Keith Magnuson in the right corner of the Chicago zone, wheeled, took three big strides back toward the blue line, then snapped the puck past Esposito at a sharp angle from twenty feet out.

The Tide Turns

Within minutes it became obvious that the tide had turned. Chicago faltered and was penalized. The Habs swarmed in on Esposito but he held, and The Forum fans began to wonder if perhaps the Canadiens weren't destined to win this one. At 13:44 Pappin was hit with a double penalty that would keep him off the ice for four minutes. Despite the one-man advantage the Canadiens could not score. During that stretch White and Stapleton, who was playing with fifty stitches in his face (the result of being cut by a skate), were tremendous.

Then, at 16:03, Bobby Hull was penalized and Montreal had a two-man advantage. For the next minute-and-a-half the Canadiens applied tremendous pressure. But with Mikita, White and Stapleton in front of him, Esposito held firm. At one point the Canadiens actually skated carousel-fashion in front of Tony, unloading a series of shots that either he or his defensemen blocked. Peter Mahovlich, watching in disbelief on the Montreal bench, slammed his stick against the ice.

Finally, just ten seconds before Pappin was due back on the ice, Frank Mahovlich circled to a spot directly in front of the Chicago net and 55 feet out. He fired the puck through a screen of players milling in front of Esposito and his goal tied the game at 2-all. Had the Hawks hung on for another ten seconds, the course of the Stanley Cup final might have been changed. Of such moments are Stanley Cups won and lost.

Controlling the Play

At the start of the third period the 17,441 fans jammed into The Forum that Sunday afternoon let out a roar. The Habs controlled play and their every move met with the approval of their fans—with one exception. Defenseman Terry Harper, who had been victimized on Bobby Hull's goal in the first period, was still being booed.

"At first I wasn't aware of the crowd being on me," Harper said later, "but, you know, I guess it does bother my playing."

In this instance, however, the jeers and catcalls lit a fire under him. Six-and-a-half minutes into the third period he started a rush from his own zone. He carried the puck across mid-ice and into the Chicago end, went around Magnuson and shot the puck from the right side, around the boards, to the left-hand corner.

"I picked it up there again," Harper said, "and then Stan Mikita tried to hit me, but I got away from him. Then Magnuson had another try, and I bumped him and then went back for the puck. I looked out in front and saw both Cournoyer and Ferguson all alone and I couldn't believe it."

Harper gave the puck to Cournoyer and he shot it by the helpless Esposito. The crowd went wild. The cheers were for Harper. The game was Montreal's. Frank Mahovlich scored again at 12:13, but that goal was just icing on the cake. In that final period Chicago managed just four shots on goal. In the last seven minutes or so the Chicago defense broke down completely. Only some superlative goaltending by Esposito kept the score respectable. The Canadiens were back in the Stanley Cup series.

When game number four started, the temperature in The Forum was 82 degrees. Outside it was 75 degrees. What transpired over the next 60 minutes of play was probably best described by Stan Mikita: "I don't think we worked hard enough to get warm and feel the heat," he said.

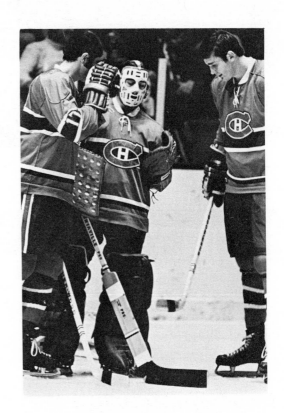

Reay, however, was still certain that Chicago could regain its advantage in game five on home ice. MacNeil and the Canadiens were just as certain that they could beat the Hawks in Chicago and then wrap up the series in the sixth game in Montreal.

Certainly the fourth game was the most one-sided of the series. Peter Mahovlich scored first for Montreal, tipping in Terry Harper's point shot at the one-minute mark. Mikita tied it for Chicago two minutes later with Beliveau off the ice. Three minutes later Beliveau put the Canadiens ahead to stay and a goal by Guy Lapointe ten minutes after that made it a 3—1 game at the end of the first period. It could have been 6—1.

Montreal's forwards and defensemen hit their Chicago counterparts almost at will. At one point Magnuson was rammed into the boards by Houle, Leon Rochefort and Houle again. Neither Magnuson nor any of his teammates fought back. The Canadiens had sixteen shots on goal, the Hawks had ten.

Nine minutes into the second period, rookie Rick Foley tried to shoot the puck across his own blue line and instead put it onto the stick of Cournoyer, who had just stepped out of the penalty box. The speedy Montrealer cruised in on Esposito and it was 4—1. Dennis Hull got that one back three minutes later, but Cournoyer scored again at 15:53 to make it 5—2. And that's the way the game ended.

The scoreless third period was notable only for a few skirmishes, the most serious between Danny O'Shea and Phil Roberto, and for the fact that Montreal fans kept breaking into an old-time Forum fight song, "Les Canadiens Sont La" (The Canadiens Are Here). One factor in the game that would prove more significant as the series wore on was Bobby Hull's being limited to two shots on goal by his young shadow, Rejean Houle.

"They Deserve to Win"

Billy Reay probably summed up the fourth game best when he said, "They deserved to win. They outskated us and played better hockey. I'm not complaining about our club but the Canadiens were just too good."

A pre-mustachioed J. C. Tremblay.

Most hockey observers now agreed that the Canadiens would win the Cup. They had momentum and confidence. Dryden had withstood the pressure and played extremely well. Montreal's offense and defense had meshed in games three and four. Chicago, on the other hand, and particularly its defense, looked tired and sluggish. Jarrett and Magnuson had been especially disappointing and there were reports, angrily denied by Reay, that Esposito was playing with an assortment of injuries. So, proving again that anything can happen in Stanley Cup play, Chicago turned around and defeated Montreal, 2–0. The Hawks did it largely on the play of Magnuson, Jarrett and Esposito, with a little inspirational help from Bobby Hull, who started hitting Canadiens early and often.

Esposito had 31 saves, the most important being the one against Jacques Lemaire early in the third period when a goal would have put Montreal back into the game. Lemaire cruised in on a breakaway and tried to get Esposito down on the ice. But Tony stayed up, blocked the shot with his chest and steered the rebound to the boards. Jarrett, meanwhile, was hitting people, handling the puck effectively in his own zone and moving it well on offense. As for the goal-scoring, Chicago got its first midway in the first period when Dennis Hull converted a goalmouth pass from Cliff Koroll.

"The Hulls did all the work on the first goal," Koroll said later. "Bobby fed me the puck at the blue line. I went deep around Laperriere and passed out into the slot. Dennis had to muscle two Canadiens out of the way to reach the pass and score. His was the major effort."

Koroll scored the second goal, at 11:26 of the second period. "Stan (Mikita) fed the puck out to Dennis (Hull) from behind the Montreal net and he fired from the left side," Koroll related. "I don't know whether the puck hit Dryden or a Montreal defenseman but it came right to me about twenty feet from the net. It was on end but I had enough time to knock it down and get control and there was plenty of room at the goal to put it through."

Over in the Montreal dressing room Al MacNeil wasn't saying much, but Henri Richard was. "He's the worst coach I ever played for in my whole career," Henri told newsmen. He complained about MacNeil's juggling of lines and players during the fifth game and the fact that he

had been given little ice time after the first period.

"I always gave 100 percent, I never loafed and I didn't deserve to be benched," Richard continued. "I'm paid to play. We had three sets of lines when we won Tuesday night (the fourth game). What gives him the right to change it all? It's about time someone said what everyone on the team is thinking. How can you expect us to win like that?"

Richard concluded his blast at MacNeil by saying, "It may be easy to win games by frequent line changes with a club like the Voyageurs, but it doesn't work like that in the National Hockey League."

MacNeil reacted by pointing out that no player had criticized him after the victories over Boston and Minnesota and the two wins over the Hawks. "Why get excited?" MacNeil asked. "In this business you get used to these things from players who are unhappy at being benched or not getting enough ice time."

General manager Sam Pollock said, "Richard is a great competitor, so is MacNeil. These things happen."

The next day a semi-penitent Richard said he should have kept his mouth shut. It was a situation impossible to ignore, but everyone on the team tried to minimize the rift. Instead, they hoped that Richard's comments might light a fire and give the players added incentive for the next two games—both of which the Canadiens had to win if they were to regain the Stanley Cup and atone for the ignominious 1969–70 season.

A Classic Game

The sixth game, at The Forum, was a Stanley Cup classic; hockey at its best and most exciting. To begin with, the game included the first penalty shot in Stanley Cup history. It was awarded to Frank Mahovlich at 4:43 of the first period.

"The Big M" was chasing a loose puck deep in the Chicago zone with no one but Esposito to beat. Esposito came out of his net, trying to beat Mahovlich to the puck. When he saw he would lose the race and leave an empty net for Mahovlich to shoot at, Esposito threw his stick at the puck and referee Art Skov immediately signaled for the historic penalty shot.

And so, in the sudden stillness of The Forum, in the opening minutes of that crucial sixth game, one of hockey's most feared shooters went one-on-one against one of hockey's finest goalies.

Esposito won the duel.

"Esposito came out earlier than I expected, and then he started to go back, and I shot too early," Frank said later. "It hit his stick. It was a good shot, but it could have been higher. It would have been better if I had 'moved' him first. I should have gone in slower and made him move first."

"I moved out at him as soon as he got to the blue line," Esposito said, "and then I moved back. I just wanted to make sure I didn't make the first move."

From that point on Chicago forced the play. Pappin scored at 11:25 with Peter Mahovlich and Magnuson in the penalty box. It was a brilliant individual effort. Pappin went around Lemaire and Lapointe and beat Dryden from close-in. But Cournoyer tied the game a minute and eight seconds later, with "The Big M" and "Le Gros Bill" assisting. The period ended with the score tied, but Chicago had the better of the play, outshooting Montreal, 11–5.

At the start of the second period Montreal took temporary control. Three minutes into the period Lemaire capped a Montreal rush with a shot into the net. But the goal was disallowed because Stapleton had knocked the net from its moorings—intentionally or otherwise. "I would gladly have taken the penalty," Stapleton said later. But there was none.

At 5:04, Peter Mahovlich put Montreal ahead. Still, Chicago kept pressing and soon regained the edge in play. In all, the Hawks had fourteen shots on goal that second period, while Montreal had only six. Two of Chicago's shots beat Dryden. The first was a 35-foot slapper by Chico Maki at 17:40 and the second by Pappin at 18:38. Pappin's goal was the result of an outstanding solo effort. Skating right to left inside the Montreal zone he went around Terry Harper, faked Laperriere and beat Dryden with a backhander. The Canadiens were twenty minutes from elimination.

The first five minutes of the third period were fairly even. Then, after a Chicago "icing," Angotti and Beliveau faced-off to the right of Esposito. The puck rolled free and out toward the blue line. Bill White put down his stick to capture it.

"The puck bounced on me," he said later. "I couldn't get my stick on it."

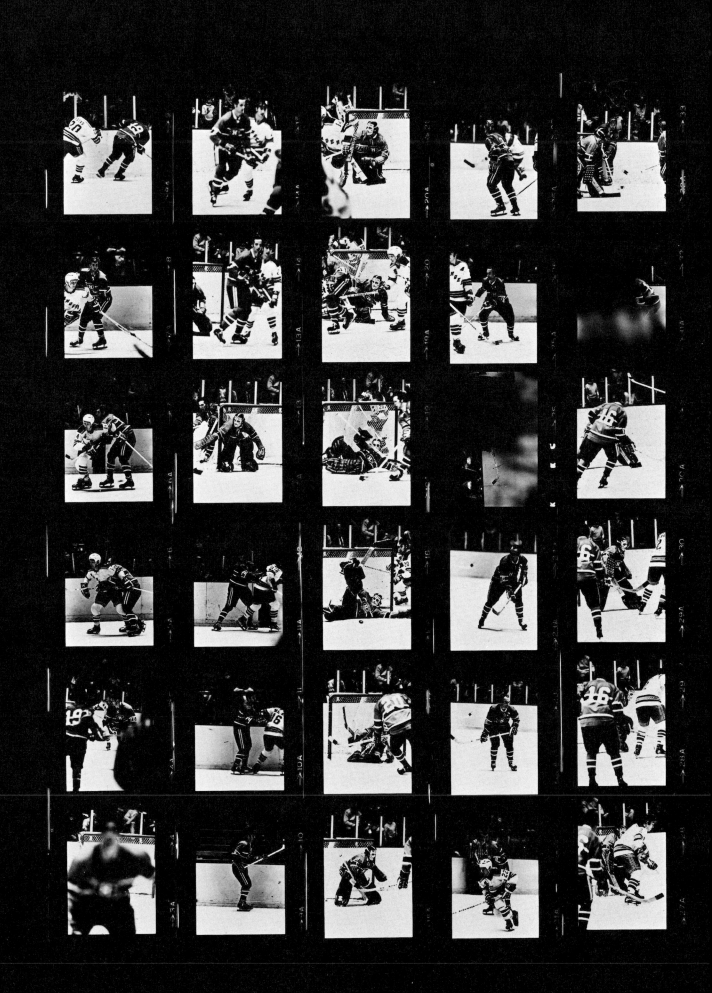

Guy Lafleur looks for a teammate and pursues Walt Tkaczuk.

A Stanley Cup Record

Frank Mahovlich got the puck, went around White and shot. Esposito blocked the puck and it rolled free. Stapleton went for it but "The Big M" got there first and shot into the empty corner of the net. The goal was Frank's fourteenth of the playoffs, a Stanley Cup record.

At 8:04, Rejean Houle was penalized for holding Bobby Hull and Chicago had a golden opportunity to regain the lead. At 8:50, in a face-off in Chicago ice just inside the blue line, Lou Angotti failed to get a clean draw and the puck bounced free. Chicago players became entangled with one another. Frank Mahovlich reached the puck first and passed it to his brother, breaking in all alone. Peter Mahovlich shot. The puck caught the net. The Forum exploded. And that's the way it ended, 4–3, Canadiens.

"I thought we had the hockey game and blew it," Reay said later. "We let in two goals on a couple of mistakes. We deserved to win and we didn't. It's an awful way to lose a hockey game. We seemed to have them on the hook today and we let 'em off."

The Telling Game

So, after 97 games for the Canadiens (78 during the regular season plus 19 in the playoffs) and 95 for the Black Hawks, the whole 1970–71 campaign came down to one final match. The Hawks were favored, primarily because of the home-ice advantage, but also because of lingering doubts that the MacNeil-Richard rift had indeed been healed. Publicly, the Canadiens were presenting a united front. Privately, well, no one could really tell.

When the teams took the ice for game number seven the temperature inside Chicago Stadium was in the low 80's. The ice was soft and the players obviously tense and tired. Happily for the National Hockey League the game was being televised nationally in the United States by CBS. This, on a Tuesday night, meant tremendous prime-time exposure. What millions of television viewers and the 20,000 fans in Chicago Stadium witnessed during 60 minutes of play was not hockey at its best, but certainly hockey at its most exciting.

From the opening face-off, Chicago carried the play. Only Dryden prevented a Hawk runaway in that first period. First, he stopped Stan Mikita at point-blank range with a kick save, and then moments later smothered a close-in follow shot by Eric Nesterenko. Later in the period he snaked out his long right leg to deflect a screen shot from the point by Keith Magnuson. Montreal, meanwhile, was having trouble getting organized. Esposito was tested, but not severely.

At 17:35, Rejean Houle was detected holding Bobby Hull and sent to the penalty box for two minutes. With his team shorthanded, Dryden stopped Jim Pappin on a close-in shot. Seconds later Bobby Hull fired a slap shot from the right point. Dryden used his stick to deflect it. When Hull's shot made contact with Dryden's stick it sounded like a rifle shot. Cliff Koroll captured the rebound and fed the puck back to Hull, still stationed at the right point. He unloaded again. Dryden went flopping across the crease to make sure he had the left-hand corner covered.

Hull's shot went wide but the puck rocketed off the boards behind the net and went straight to Dennis Hull, who was positioned in the left face-off circle. He shot as Dryden skidded back across the crease. The puck struck Dryden on the shoulder and glanced into the net. At 19:12 of the first period the Hawks had the lead.

Early in the second period, with the Hawks down two men and Montreal down one man, Lemaire captured the puck five feet in front of Esposito and flipped a back-hander for the corner. Somehow Esposito got his right leg out and blocked it. This seemed to inspire Chicago and for the next few minutes the Hawks swarmed around the Montreal net. Finally, after a face-off deep in Montreal ice, Doug Jarrett shot the puck behind the net. Pit Martin outhustled two Canadiens for it and centered to Danny O'Shea. He fired from 25 feet out and the Hawks had a 2–0 lead. That was at 7:33, and with Esposito seemingly in top form and the rest of the Hawks playing exceptionally well, it appeared that two goals would be enough for a Chicago win.

Yvan Cournoyer yells for a pass.

Goal Number One

Then the roof fell in on the Black Hawks. Montreal got its first goal when Jacques Lemaire, skating leisurely toward the Chicago blue line, suddenly fired a slap shot toward the Chicago net from 80 feet out. Esposito flopped to his knees. But the puck kept rising and sailed over his right shoulder and into the net.

"I saw it all the way," Esposito said later. "I just missed it."

The goal stunned the Chicago crowd and the Chicago players as well. You could almost feel the confidence starting to drain out of them, as if someone had suddenly pulled the plug in a bathtub full of water. Lemaire's goal came at 14:18. At 18:20 the Habs tied the score.

Nesterenko and Lemaire chased the puck into the right corner of the Chicago zone. Nesterenko reached it first and shot it toward Bill White behind the Chicago goal. The puck hit the side of the net and bounced back to Lemaire. He centered to Henri Richard and the "Pocket Rocket" beat Esposito at point-blank range.

As the third period started there again was that feeling of inevitability, the feeling that the Canadiens were not to be denied. At 2:34 Henri Richard scored what proved to be the winning goal. He did so by flashing across the Chicago blue line on the left side. Then, after eluding Magnuson's frantic dive, Richard drew Esposito to the ice before flipping a shot over the sprawled goalie's shoulder. After that the game was in Dryden's hands. Ten minutes from the end of the game he made what has been described as "the stop of the season."

Jim Pappin had taken a pass that left him wide open eight feet in front of the Montreal net. He shot and then raised his stick in celebration, so certain was he that the puck was in.

"I was moving across the net, following the course of the pass," Dryden explained. "I really wasn't moving toward Pappin's shot. Pappin's shot hit me low on the right pad. I was fortunate."

Montreal's 16th Stanley Cup

Ten minutes later it was all over. The Canadiens had won their 16th Stanley Cup since the formation of the National Hockey League in 1917. It may have been the most satisfying Stanley Cup of all.

In the Montreal dressing room there was unrestrained joy. Some players were laughing, others were crying. Three of the Canadiens had hoisted MacNeil onto their shoulders and carried him off the ice. In the dressing room MacNeil and Richard embraced. All was forgiven in the flush of victory.

"This is my best ever," proclaimed Beliveau. "The one I enjoyed the most because we did what a lot of people didn't think we could do, beat the Bruins in Boston and the Hawks in Chicago."

"I am glad we won," Richard said. "It was a helluva relief after what I said the last time we were here. I should have kept my mouth shut. But I just lost my temper, it was one of those things I'll always be sorry for. Now maybe everybody will forget."

"Sure I was worried but I had confidence, too," Mac-Neil said. "I was certain that they could win this seventh game in Chicago. These fellows are quite a hockey team."

Finally, Toe Blake, who had coached the Canadiens to eight Stanley Cup victories, said, "This is the greatest victory since I have been around the Canadiens. These fellows won every series on the other team's ice. That's an incredible feat, and they came from behind in several games, snatched victory from teams who thought they had won. No team has ever shown more heart under pressure."

When the Canadiens returned to Montreal in the early morning after their night of triumph, 3,000 fans were waiting to greet them. The next day a half-million Montrealers cheered their heroes during a motorcade from The Forum to City Hall. The biggest cheers were for Beliveau and Richard and for Dryden, who had been chosen to receive the Conn Smythe Trophy as the Most Valuable Player in the Stanley Cup playoffs.

There were cheers for Al MacNeil, too, but a few weeks later he was replaced as coach by Scotty Bowman, one-time coach and general-manager of the St. Louis Blues.

It was, all in all, quite an ending to quite a year.

the Montreal Mystique

At one point during his college years, Ken Dryden encountered a passage from Robert Browning's poem *Andrea Del Sarto*:

Ah, but a man's reach should exceed his grasp,
Or what's a heaven for?

Few words could better depict the inspiration behind the overwhelming and stirring seven-game 1971 Stanley Cup triumphs engineered by Dryden and his Montreal Canadien teammates over the supposedly indomitable Boston Bruins, the Minnesota North Stars and the Chicago Black Hawks.

Ken Dryden falls to his left knee while Guy Lafleur clears the crease of an enemy forward. ▶

Magnificent competitors such as Jean Beliveau, Henri Richard and J. C. Tremblay, to name just a few, reached within themselves to extract the last bits of energy required for the superhuman effort. And extract it they did.

And when it appeared that the Canadiens had finally and sorrowfully drained themselves dry, the Mahovliches, John Ferguson, Terry Harper and Yvon Cournoyer did, in Browning's terms, once more exceed their grasp. The result was what amounted to heaven for hockey's Flying Frenchmen.

More than any other hockey club—or any professional team, for that matter—Les Canadiens ooze with a distillation of pride and tradition that far exceeds the norm. To the unknowing, it may sound like corn, but those familiar with Le Club de Hockey Canadien realize that the baton of Georges Vezina has been passed on first to Howie Morenz, then to Maurice (Rocket) Richard and then to Captain Jean Beliveau, as well as to the indefatigable Henri Richard.

While the hockey world, with precious few exceptions, was writing them off, the Canadiens were busy believing in themselves. On the eve of the seventh game against Boston, Terry Harper, an occasionally clumsy but always battling defenseman, told a newsman who had earlier predicted a rout by Boston in the series, that he believed the Habs would prevail.

"I think we have the better team," said Harper quite simply. "If we play our best, even if they play their best, we will win."

How right he was.

It takes more than an overdose of guts to drop behind the Bruins in a seventh game at Boston Garden and then surmount the deficit to capture the game. It takes exceptional fortitude for a Lilliputianlike skater such as Henri Richard, who stands five feet seven and weighs 160 pounds, to outfight and humiliate six-foot-one, 180-pound Wayne Cashman as the Pocket Rocket did in that furious finale.

But the most stirring demonstration of the Canadiens' valor developed when the Bruins scored their second goal early in the final period to pull to within 2 of tying. Now the supposedly invincible Boston sextet would capture the momentum and bulldoze over the faltering visitors. Instead, it was the Canadiens who skated harder than ever.

Everybody Skates

"When everybody skates," said Richard, "everything comes easier." And skate they did. Yet, it was far from easy. Several times the Boston infantry penetrated to the lip of Montreal's trenches only to be repulsed by Dryden, who remained militantly implacable.

No one knows what strange jitterbugging goes on within that young man's metabolism, but outwardly Dryden appears as serene as the Statue of Liberty, especially when he gently rests his masked face on the tip of his stick during face-off breaks.

This is the same Dryden who played a grand total of six regular NHL games before entering the meat grinder that is the Stanley Cup playoffs. Only six regular NHL games, and the McGill University law student took the best missiles hockey's highest-scoring juggernaut could fire and defused them in seven games. It made the word "upset" seem terribly inappropriate. After Minnesota was deflated it was the Black Hawks' turn. The series seesawed back and forth until Chicago took a 3–2 lead. And when, in the sixth game, Chicago took a 3–2 lead in the third period, it appeared that they had the Cup. But the Mystique was there and victory was snatched from the jaws of defeat. And it held in the final game when the Black Hawks assaulted the Montreal zone in waves desperately attempting to score the tying goal.

And when, in that final game, the Canadiens protected their fragile lead until the clock ticked off another Stanley Cup victory for Les Habitants, that indefinable quality was still with them.

Sam Pollock– Champion Builder

The immediate past of the Montreal Canadiens—and their immediate future—is really wrapped up in one man, general manager Sam Pollock. He has been described by his friends as shrewd, tough and able, and by his enemies as a corporate in-fighter who was extremely lucky to make it to the top. The truth probably lies somewhere in between. At any rate, during Pollock's reign in the Montreal front offce—which began in 1964—the Canadiens have gone from top to bottom and back to the top again. It is difficult to blame Pollock for Montreal's slide. It is equally difficult not to credit him with Montreal's rise.

For example, soon after six expansion teams were admitted into the National Hockey League in the 1967–68 season, they found Pollock quite willing to provide them with players, for a price. The prime recipients were the Minnesota North Stars and the St. Louis Blues. As things developed, Minnesota and St. Louis met in the West Division finals of Stanley Cup play. The Blues won, met the Canadiens and lost in four-straight games.

Still, the 1967–68 campaign had worked out so well for all three teams that Minnesota's general-manager, Wren Blair, was moved to say, "Look at it this way. Sam's big club made the final, and two of his farm teams fought it out to meet the big club." Pollock responded by saying, "I'm glad to see the teams we dealt with got their money's worth."

Marc Tardif hurls his shot, then falls to the ice.

Since then Pollock has continued to deal with the expansionists, and while it may not always have been profitable for the newcomers, there is little doubt that Pollock has done extremely well at the trading block. He has done so well, in fact, that by the conclusion of the 1970–71 campaign he had acquired, through trades, ten first-round and three second-round amateur draft choices for the next three seasons. As a result the Canadiens were able to acquire Guy Lafleur in the 1971 draft. Lafleur was regarded as the cream of the current crop and Montreal got him because it held California's first-round choice. Since the Golden Seals finished with the worst record in hockey, the Canadiens had first pick.

Montreal also held Minnesota's first-round choice and Los Angeles' second-round selection. In June 1972 the Canadiens will have four first-round picks—their own, plus those of Minnesota, Los Angeles and California. And they'll also have the number two choices of Minnesota and L.A. In 1973 Montreal will have its own first-round selection, along with those of California and Minnesota.

The Smartest Man in any Front-Office Job

Of such things are hockey dynasties made. And because of such things Sam Pollock is held in high esteem by many of hockey's more astute observers. One knowledgeable observer has called him the smartest man now connected with hockey in any front-office job.

Ironically, when Pollock first moved into the Montreal front office he was regarded by some as an interloper who would lead the Canadiens down the road to destruction. Given the circumstances of Pollock's promotion to the post of general manager, the reaction was understandable.

For one thing, he succeeded Frank Selke, who was as much a part of the Canadiens' history as The Forum. To get the job, Pollock had to outfight Ken Reardon, who was not only a vice-president of the club at the time but had been one of their best defensemen ever. Finally, Pollock was only thirty-eight at the time of his appointment, and there were those who felt that he wasn't ready for the task ahead, even though he had been with the Montreal organization since 1950 and director of the team's farm system since 1958. Pollock, however, never for a moment doubted that he was ready. And since his ascendancy into the front office he has swung a few of the best trades in the history of the NHL.

In 1969, for example, Pollock acquired Peter Mahovlich from the Detroit Red Wings. Anyone familiar with the Stanley Cup playoffs is fully aware of just how valuable Mahovlich has become to the Canadiens. To get him Pollock gave up Doug Piper and Garry Monahan. Monahan is now with Toronto. At last look Piper was buried in the minors.

When it was suggested to Pollock that he really pulled one off on the Wings, he bristled. "We simply liked Pete. We got something we wanted. They (the Red Wings) got something they wanted. Maybe we were fortunate."

Midway through the 1970–71 season Pollock acquired Peter's brother Frank, who rates as one of the great scorers of hockey. Pollock also got Frank from Detroit.

"Frank is a superstar—always has been," Pollock explains. "They don't come along every day. So I gave up three players to get him. The Leafs once gave up five men to get Max Bentley. If I gave up three to get Frank, I guess I'm entitled to think I'm justified."

The three players Pollock parted with were Mickey Redmond, Bill Collins and Guy Charron.

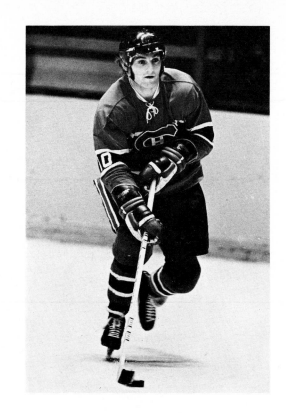

Keeping the Team Afloat

Pollock's talents, however, go far beyond some of his more spectacular deals. He has done what few others could have done, namely, kept the Canadiens afloat during one of the stormiest periods in the team's history.

What lay ahead for Pollock was not evident during his first season in the front office. Montreal finished first in 1965–66, swept Toronto in the first round of Stanley Cup play and then defeated Detroit in a six-game final. The following season the Canadiens were without "Boom Boom" Geoffrion, who had left to coach and play for the Quebec Aces. Jean Beliveau almost lost the sight of one eye when he was hit by a stick and goaltender Gump Worsley was hospitalized with a concussion after being struck on the head with a hard-boiled egg thrown from the balcony of Madison Square Garden.

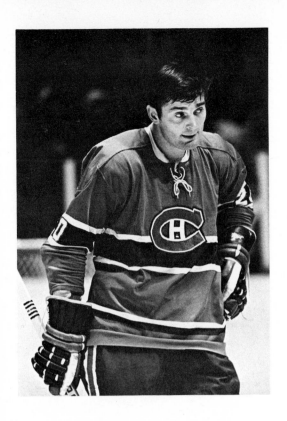

Still, the Canadiens managed to finish second and they swept the New York Rangers in the first-round of Stanley Cup play. But in the final round they lost to the Maple Leafs in six games. Montreal regained the Cup in 1968. But Toe Blake, regarded by many as the finest coach in the history of professional hockey, resigned after that season. If Pollock has one major failing, it is his inability to find a worthy replacement. Blake's immediate successor was thirty-one-year-old Claude Ruel.

"Plain and simple, Ruel was Pollock's prodigy," Maurice Richard, one of Pollock's more outspoken critics, has written. "Ruel had worked for Pollock ever since he had been a junior and Pollock wanted a man who knew what he (Pollock) wanted with no back talk."

Richard also blames Pollock for Blake's departure. He says that with Pollock as general-manager, the whole atmosphere of the Montreal organization changed radically.

"Hockey wasn't as much fun as it had been," Richard has said. "And I'm sure Toe Blake felt that. I think he would have quit a lot sooner than he did but Pollock kept urging him to stay. Toe didn't like the change in the organization any more than I did, although he wasn't the kind who would come out and say so. He wasn't wild about Pollock either and he finally left the team."

At any rate, the Canadiens again won the Stanley Cup during Ruel's first year, but cracks in the team were beginning to show. That, plus the emergence of the New York Rangers and Boston Bruins as legitimate contenders, set Pollock upon a course that at first glance appeared to be suicidal. Simply put, Pollock decided to break up Les Canadiens.

He traded Bobby Rousseau and Ted Harris to Minnesota and sent Ralph Backstrom and Dick Duff to Los Angeles. Worsley quit the Canadiens in a huff and was dispatched to Minnesota. What transpired in 1969–70 earned Pollock a great many "I told you so's." Pollock then raised a few more eyebrows by cleaning out the Montreal farm system. He sent Jude Drouin to Minnesota, where he performed extremely well. Drouin may turn out to be another one of Pollock's rare mistakes, like Tony Esposito. But at the same time he also traded away other players who have not made much of a splash with their new teams—men like Jack Norris, Larry Mickey, Ernie Hicke and Fran Huck. In return Pollock received those treasured draft choices.

A Realist

"Sam Pollock is a realist," says Montreal *Star* columnist John Robertson. "He foresaw the end of the Canadien dynasty and accurately concluded that there wasn't a heckuva lot he could do about the Rangers and Bruins temporarily catching up and passing him. But instead of panicking and dealing for a lot of older, experienced players who might make the club a little better, but still not good enough, he decided to bide his time and set the stage for another dynasty."

Just so Montreal fans wouldn't get bored waiting around for that dynasty to happen, the Canadiens won another Stanley Cup.

Pollock took a calculated risk in easing out winning coach Al MacNeil. Even Henri Richard said after Montreal's Cup victory that he would be disappointed if MacNeil was not back to coach the team in 1971–72. But Pollock minimized his risk somewhat by bringing in Scotty Bowman, a proven winner with the St. Louis Blues.

So with a veteran and highly respected coach . . . a group of young players who have been tried and found not wanting in Stanley Cup play . . . and a pocketful of high draft choices . . . it would seem that Sam Pollock can look to the future with confidence.

In fact, it just seems possible that Pollock and the Canadiens have already embarked on still another Montreal dynasty—while no one was looking. Only time will tell.

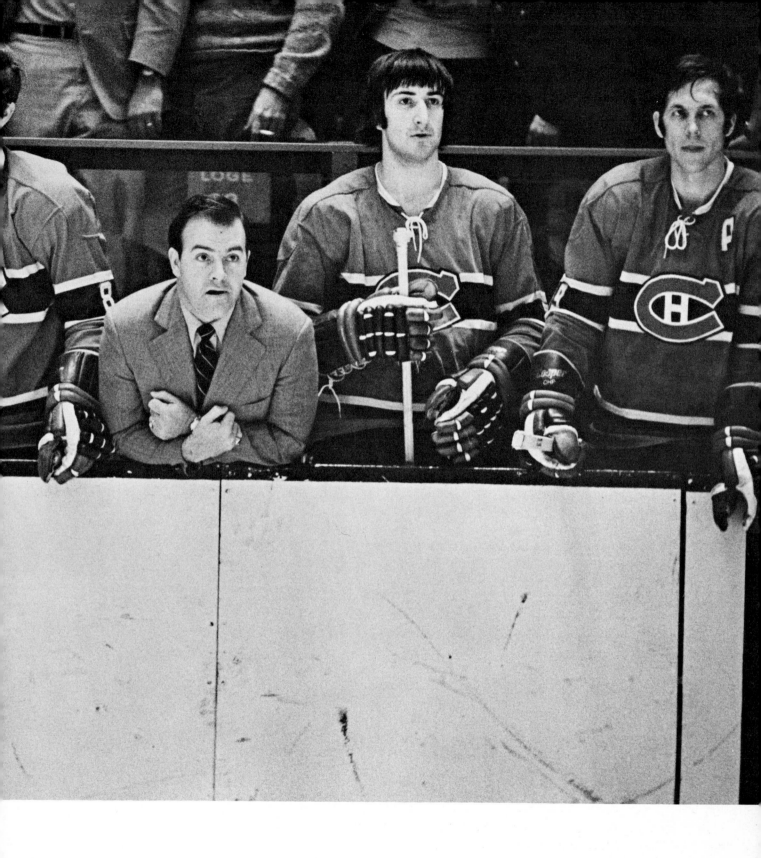

Canadiens' new coach Scotty Bowman is flanked by Larry Pleau (L), Guy Lapointe and Terry Harper.

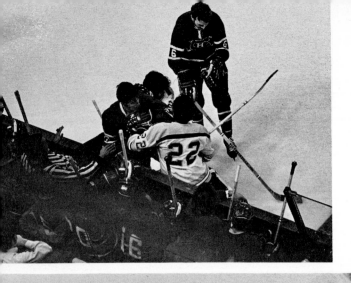

Conflict

Ted Irvine of the Rangers makes the mistake of mixing it with big Pierre Bouchard of the Canadiens. One punch by Pierre and Irvine is down for the TKO.

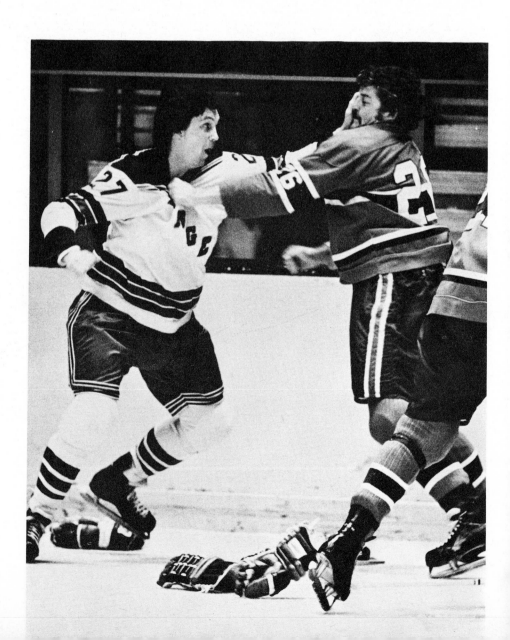

The aftermath; the winner is on the right; the loser is hidden behind Bruce MacGregor (14).

Anyone for the Minuet?

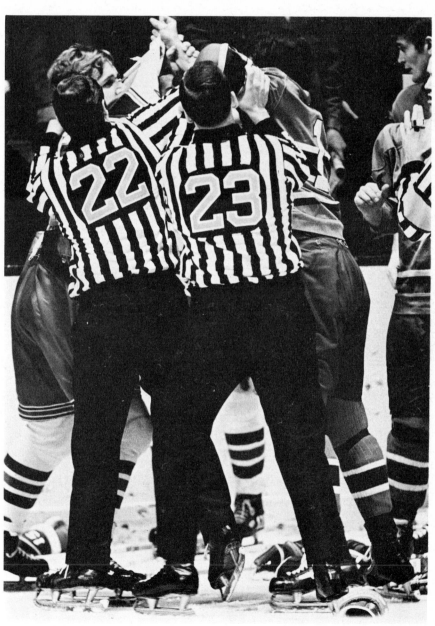

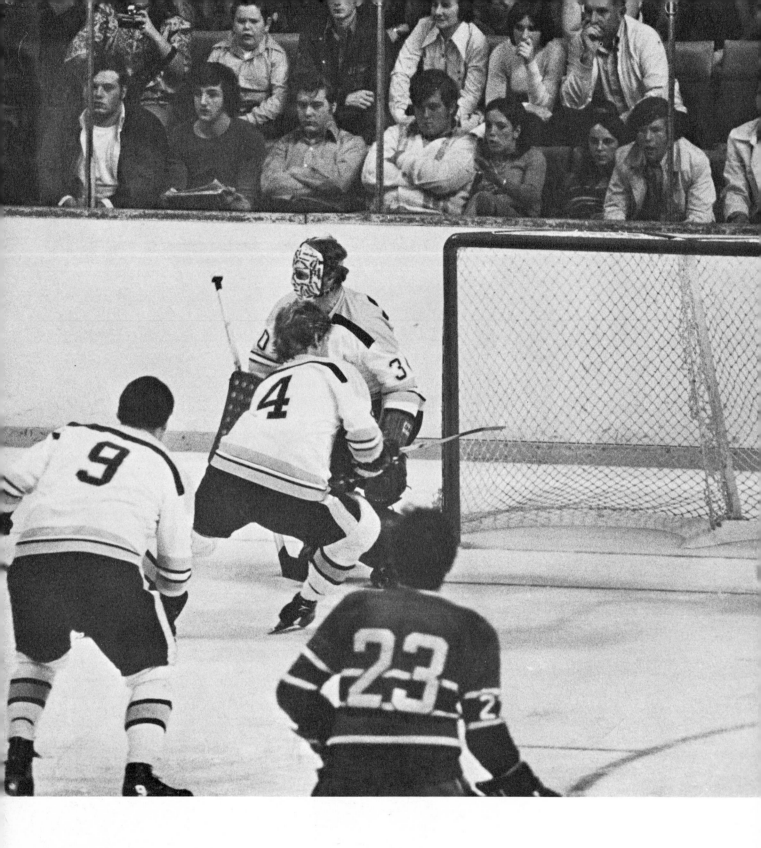

Claude Larose plants himself in front of the Boston net awaiting the pass-out.

While Bobby Orr rushes to cover Larose, the Montreal forward captures the pass with goalie Gerry Cheevers far out of position on the left.

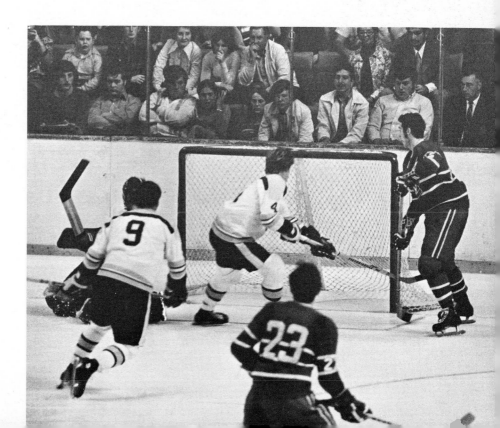

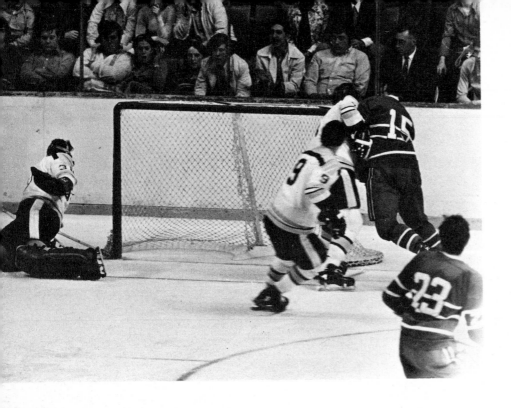

Orr arrives too late as Larose trips the
puck home.

Peter Mahovlich arrives behind the net in time to signal the goal.

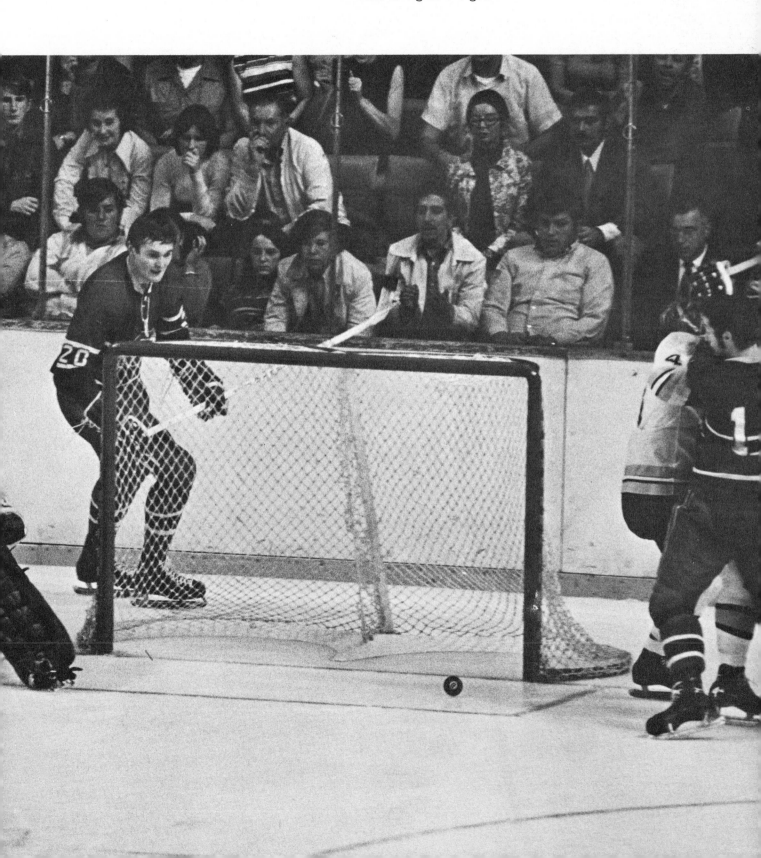

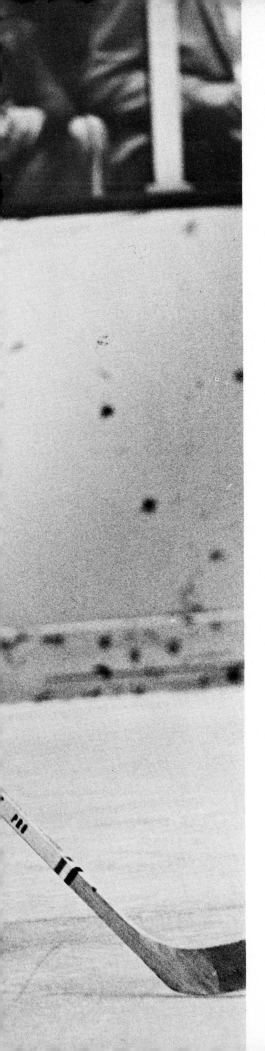

the Goalies

Goaltenders come in all sizes and shapes. Ken Dryden the Cornell University graduate, is one of the tallest in pro hockey. Teammate Phil Myre also is one of the bigger goalies as contrasted with the short and compact Rogatien Vachon.

you can't stop 'em all.

Rogatien Vachon studies the oncoming Rangers' shot.

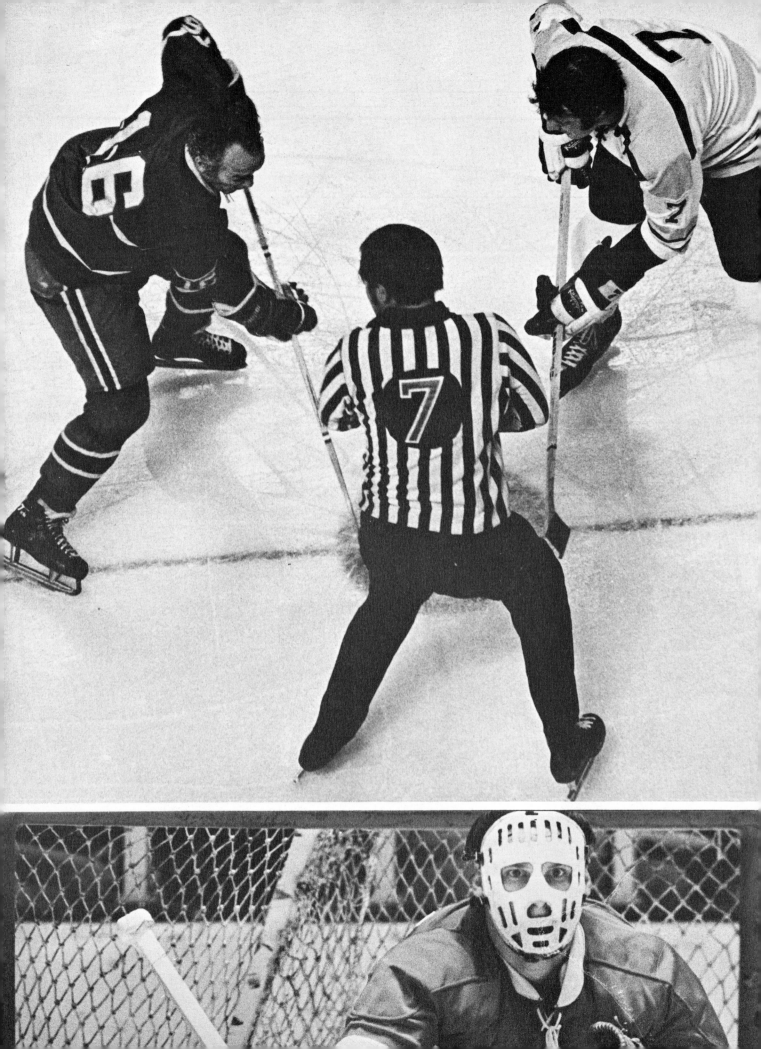

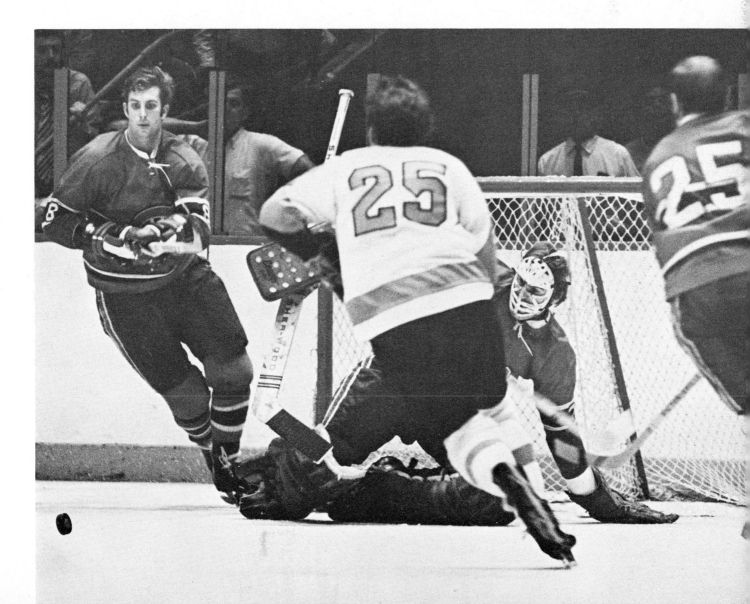

Frank Mahovlich steals the loose puck from Rangers' goalie Ed Giacomin, pushes the puck, and himself, into the net as teammates Yvan Cournoyer (center) and Peter Mahovlich shout congratulations.

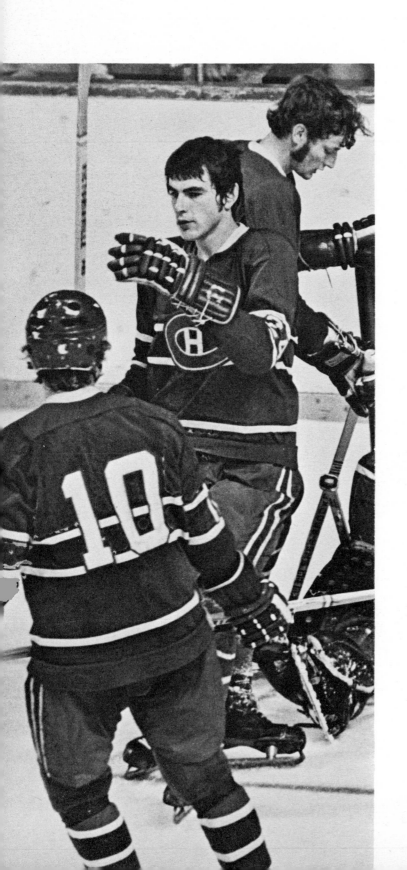

97

the "Pocket Rocket"

Small but tough, Captain Henri "Pocket Rocket" Richard has followed in the skate-steps of his brother, Maurice "The Rocket" Richard, a former Canadiens' captain.

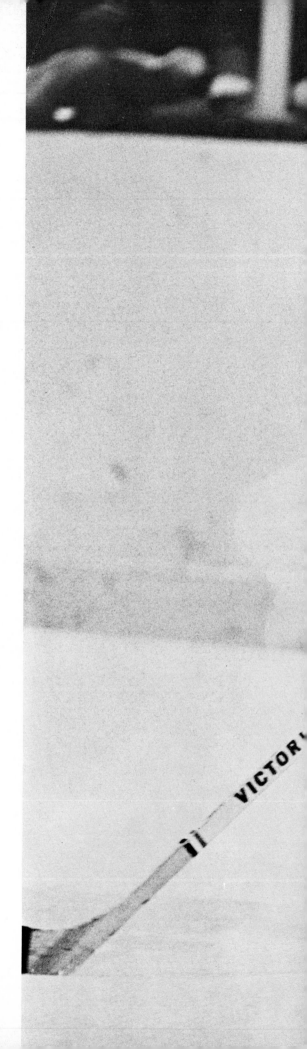

Henri Richard wins the face-off from New York's Jean Ratelle.

Henri mixes it with Ron Stewart, then a Ranger.

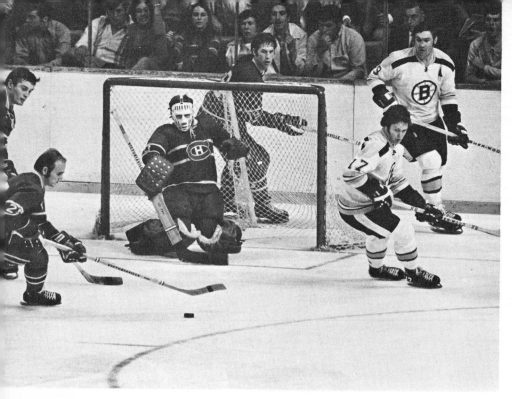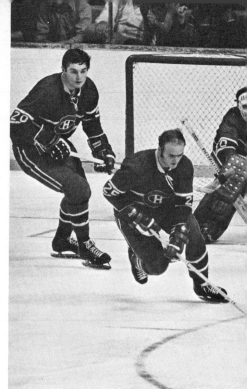

Jacques Lemaire blunts a Boston assault and
reverses to counterattack.

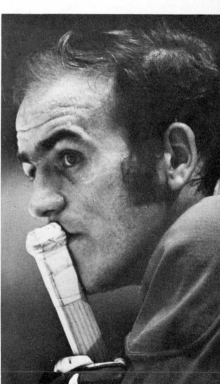

Jacques Laperriere

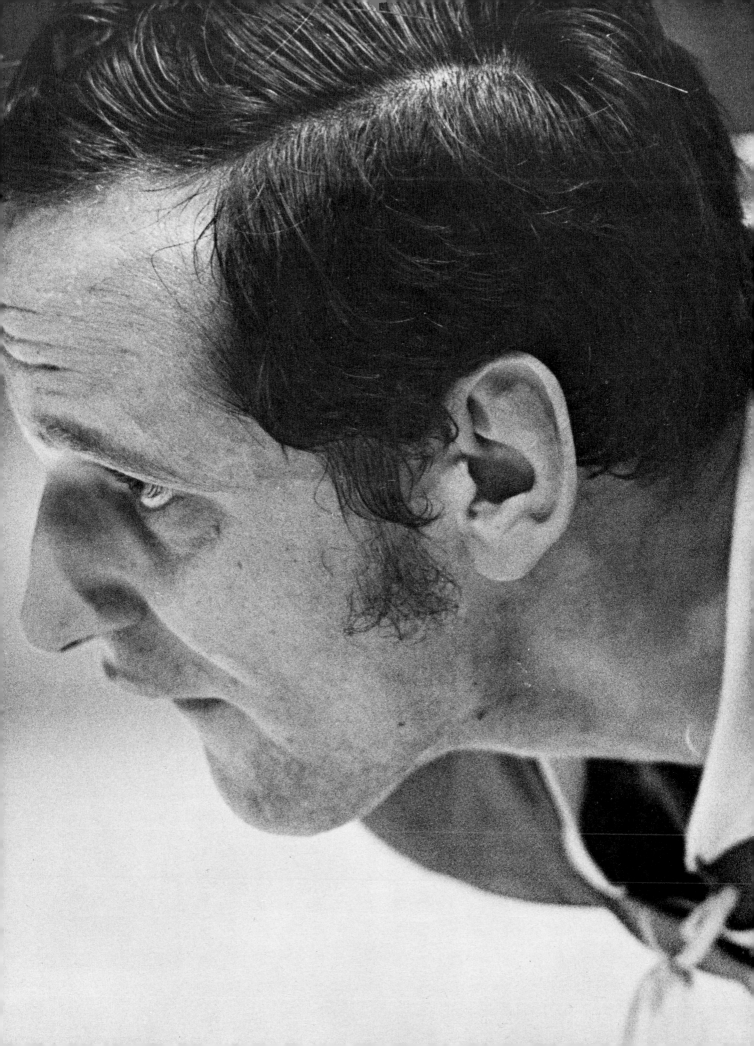

Ken Dryden makes the save.

Frank "Big M" Mahovlich, swoops toward the Rangers' goal, crowds defenseman Jim Neilson and, finally, puts the puck past goalie Ed Giacomin.

J. C. Tremblay

An All-Star defenseman, J. C. Tremblay is renowned for his superb puck control and ability to put an attack in motion.

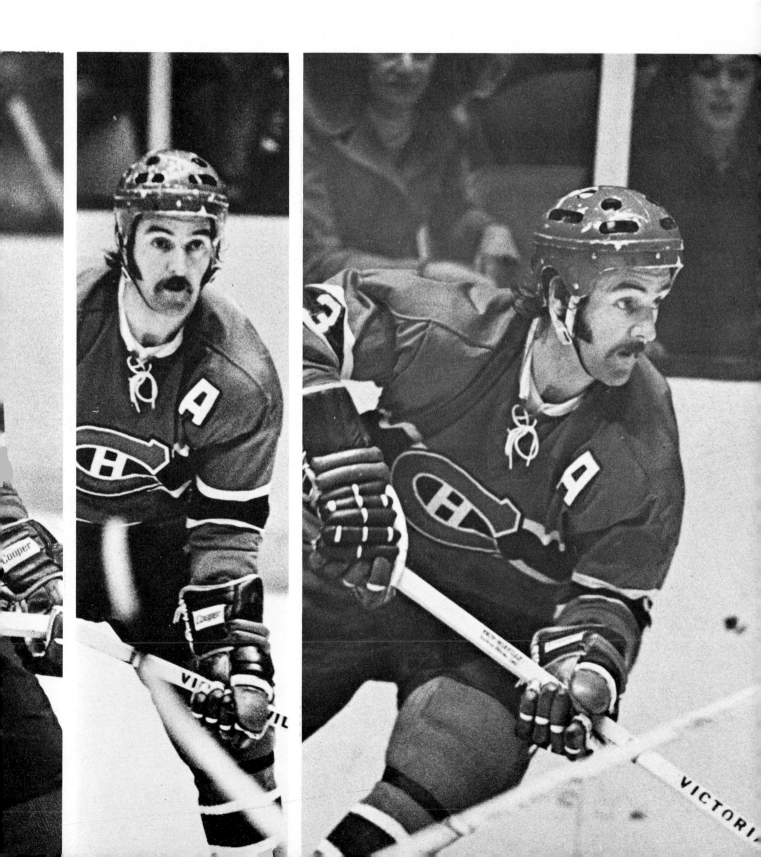

Defenseman Terry Harper is poised in front of the Canadiens' net.

Rejean Houle (14) and Captain Henri Richard.

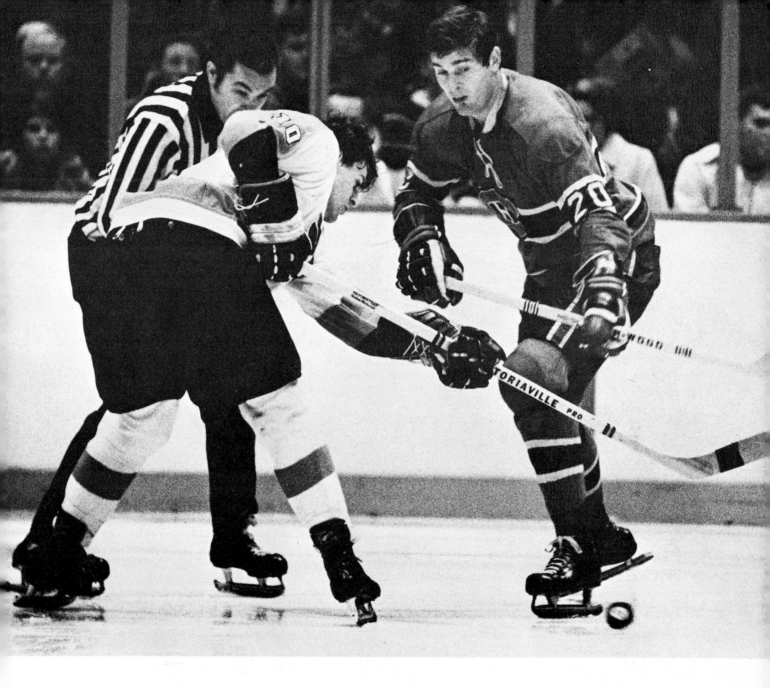

Peter Mahovlich passes to his left from the
face-off.

Peering out from behind his prison-like mask is goalie Phil Myre.

In a typical crouched position, alert Rogatien Vachon awaits a shot on goal.

Guarded by Bobby Orr, Marc Tardif awaits a
pass in front of the Boston goal.

Claude Larose whistles a shot on goal.

Guy Lafleur, the hope of the future.

Yvan Cournoyer, a Canadien; an All-Star.

126

the Defender

Terry Harper epitomizes all that a coach desires in a defensive-defenseman. He uses his size to advantage, rarely is caught out of position in the enemy zone and is an indefatigable skater.

Defenseman Terry Harper moves in to take
Phil Esposito out of the play.

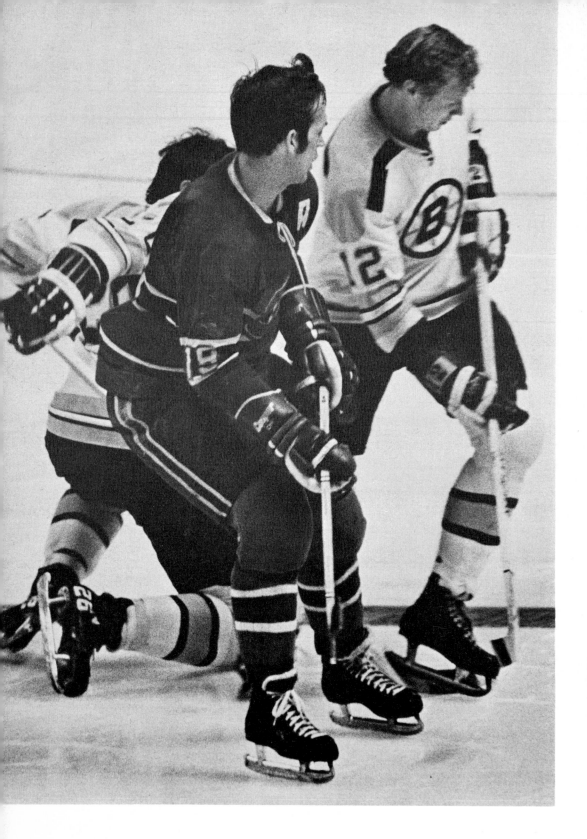

a Brief History

For those French-speaking Canadian youngsters who get up before dawn in below-zero temperatures so they can be playing hockey by sunup, the dream is to play in The Forum someday . . . to wear the bleu-blanc-et-rouge of Les Canadiens . . . and perhaps, also someday, to drink champagne from the Cup, as so many Habs have.

Montreal really won its first Stanley Cup in 1894, defeating the Ottawa Capitals, 3–1, before a crowd of 5,000 in Montreal's Victoria Rink.

At the time there were three hockey teams in the city—the Victorias, the Shamrocks and the Montreal Athletic Association, known simply as Montreal. It was Montreal, the forerunner of Les Canadiens, which won the Cup in 1894. But it was 1910 before the Canadiens were officially born. That occurred when they were granted a franchise in the National Hockey Association of Canada, which ultimately became the National Hockey League.

The Canadiens' first season was a disaster. They won only two games and lost ten. Their local rivals, the Montreal Wanderers, led the league with an 11–1 record and also won the Stanley Cup. The following season the Canadiens were second, largely because of the play of forward Newsy Lalonde and the goaltending of young Georges Vezina. In his fifteen years with the Canadiens, Vezina never missed a game; and he became so good that the NHL ultimately struck a trophy in his name, awarded each year to the netminder allowing the fewest goals during the regular season.

Thanks to Vezina, Lalonde and some other outstanding French-speaking players, the Canadiens developed a distinctive image early in their history. That image endures today.

"The Canadiens' charm is Gallic," says Peter Gzowski,

one of the most perceptive writers on the North American continent. "And the headlong, passionate way they have always played hockey has helped make them the national team of French Canada in a way no team representing all of Canada, with its diverse, unmelted ethnic strains, could hope to parallel."

The Canadiens enjoyed the first of their many highly successful seasons in 1915–16. They finished first in regular-season play, then squared off against the Portland Rosebuds, champions of the Pacific Coast Hockey Association, for the Stanley Cup. Montreal and Portland split the first four games, but as was to happen so often in the years ahead, the Canadiens won the deciding game, 2–1. Each member of the Canadiens collected $238. Each of the Portland players made the long trek home richer by $207.

The First Great Scorer

The first of the great Montreal scorers was Joe Malone, a center who joined the Canadiens in 1917. "He might have been the most prolific scorer of all time if they had played more games in those days," said Frank J. Selke, onetime managing director of the Montreal team. "It was amazing the way Joe used to get himself in position to score. In that respect his style was similar to Gordie Howe's."

Malone played in 20 of Montreal's 22 games during the 1917–18 campaign. He scored 44 goals, a mark that stood until the 1944–45 season when Maurice Richard netted 50.

"The funny thing is," Malone said, "there was more publicity about my record when Maurice Richard broke it than there was when I set it."

Despite Malone and a number of other talented players, the Canadiens did not win the Cup in the 1917–18 season, although they finished first in the league standings. In fact, the Canadiens finished no lower than third in any year through the 1924–25 season. But the 1925–26 campaign was a disaster, both personally and professionally.

It began on the night of November 28, 1925 at the Mount Royal Arena in Montreal. Pittsburgh, one of the three new American entries in the league, provided the opposition. Vezina, whose health had been growing progressively worse through the previous year, was in the Montreal nets. He had gone to the arena with a temperature of 105

degrees and had told no one about his illness. Even so, Vezina played the first period with skill and ease.

Back in the locker room between periods he sustained what was later diagnosed as an arterial hemorrhage but returned to the nets for the second period. A few minutes later Vezina collapsed on the ice.

"In the stricken arena," one observer noted, "all was silent as the limp form of the greatest of goalies was carried slowly from the ice." The following March 24 Vezina died of tuberculosis.

Enter Morenz

Without Vezina, the Canadiens finished seventh that season. As was to happen so often in Montreal history, the loss of one star foreshadowed the emergence of another, in this instance Howie Morenz.

Morenz was a center and one of the swiftest skaters ever to play in the NHL. "He was the picture player," said Nels Stewart, himself a member of the Hall of Fame. "Howie had the grace and speed to finish off plays like no one else could."

Morenz led the team for ten years beginning in the mid 1920's, a dedicated player, always determined to win. Along with another great Montreal player of that era, Aurel Joliat, he scored 270 career goals. Together, they helped write some of the brightest chapters in the history of Les Canadiens.

Starting with the 1926–27 season and continuing through 1937–38, the Canadiens finished in first place on five occasions, second three times, third in three campaigns and fourth only once. The Canadiens also won the Stanley Cup twice during that span.

The Canadiens traded Morenz to the Chicago Black Hawks just before the start of the 1934–35 season but got him back two years later. Like Vezina, he was destined for a tragic end. In a game against the Black Hawks in The Forum on the night of January 28, 1937 Morenz was checked heavily into the boards and suffered a broken leg. In the hospital he started to brood about his future. He suffered a nervous breakdown, developed heart trouble and died on March 8 at the age of thirty-six.

Morenz's funeral was held in the Montreal Forum. Andy O'Brien, a hockey writer of that time, noted, "As I walked below the north end, profound silence left an impression of emptiness, but at the promenade I stopped in breathless awe. The rink was jammed to the rafters with fans standing

motionless with heads bared."

In 1938–39 the Canadiens finished sixth. The following year they were seventh. And for the two seasons after that they were sixth again. Incredible! The mightly Canadiens, doormats of the league.

The Fabled Rocket

Yet, again, the Canadiens found the player who would lead them out of the hockey wilderness—Maurice Richard, the fabled "Rocket." Each goal that Richard scored is in the record books in black and white. What is not in the books is the Richard fire, drive and determination, the flair and dedication that inspired others and made him such a great competitor and player.

Richard joined the Canadiens in 1942 but because of injuries did not really hit his stride until the Stanley Cup playoffs in 1944. In the semifinals against Toronto, Richard scored all of Montreal's goals in a 5–1 victory. Then, in the finals against the Chicago Black Hawks, Richard scored all of Montreal's goals in a 3–1 win as Montreal swept the Hawks and won their first Stanley Cup in thirteen years.

The following season Richard set his record of 50 goals in fifty games. The Canadiens were first that season, and the following two seasons as well. They won the Stanley Cup in 1945–46, but did not win it again until 1952–53. It was another three years before the Cup was theirs again. After that the Canadiens dominated the National Hockey League as no other team had before, or is likely to again.

Beginning with the 1955–56 season, the Canadiens won five consecutive Stanley Cups. From 1957–58 through 1961–62 they finished atop the league in regular-season play. They did it with players like Richard, Beliveau, Geoffrion and Dickie Moore on offense . . . with defensemen like Harvey and Tom Johnson . . . and with the goaltending of Jacques Plante. Plus the coaching of Toe Blake.

The Canadiens have won the Stanley Cup since and they have also finished atop the league in regular-season play. But in recent years they haven't approached the pinnacle of hockey perfection they enjoyed through most of the 1950's and the early 1960's.

No matter what else happens, hockey fans know with certainty that the Flying Frenchmen will always be in the forefront of play for the League championship and the Stanley Cup.

Hockey seems to be doing the same thing for Soviet-Canadian relations that ping pong has done for Sino-U.S. affairs. Henri (Pocket Rocket) Richard gets some Russian hockey tips from Soviet Premier Alexei Kosygin at a Canadien-Vancouver game in Vancouver. (The Canadiens won.)